THE MASTER ARCHITECT SERIES II

NBBJ

Selected and Current Works

Front row, left to right: Helman, Böhm, Anderson
Back row, left to right: Hoedemaker, Pangiazio, Bain, Jonassen, Zimmerman, Wyatt

NBBJ

Selected and Current Works

First published in Australia in 1997 by
The Images Publishing Group Pty Ltd
ACN 059 734 431
6 Bastow Place, Mulgrave, Victoria, 3170
Telephone (61 3) 9561 5544 Facsimile (61 3) 9561 4860

National Library of Australia Cataloguing-in-Publication Data

    NBBJ.
       NBBJ: selected and current works.

       Bibliography.
       Includes index.
       ISBN 1 875498 54 0.
       Master Architect Series II ISSN 1320 7253

       1. NBBJ (Firm). 2. Architecture, American.
       3. Architecture, Modern—20th century—United
       States. I. Title. (Series: Master architect series. 2).

    720.973

Edited by Stephen Dobney
Designed by The Graphic Image Studio Pty Ltd,
Mulgrave, Australia
Film by Scanagraphix Australia Pty Ltd
Printing by Everbest Printing, Hong Kong

Contents

INTRODUCTION

Preface

Our vision for NBBJ is to be the best design firm in the world. Clients, their concerns, and their projects are our reason for being; our studios are the medium through which we serve them. We believe that good design always adds value: to our clients' endeavors, the users, the community, society, and the environment.

We are citizens of the world and global practitioners, deeply committed to socially and environmentally responsible design. At the same time, we practice regionally and encourage a rich diversity of beliefs, approaches, and solutions. Our team members share certain essential talents: lively intelligence, superior skills, superb training informed by a broad education, and the ability to communicate persuasively. We are creative, curious, passionate, responsible, and willing to take and share risk. We emphasize personal and professional growth, in a spirit of creativity, innovation, collaboration, and commitment.

As partners, we take honesty and integrity to be the unshakable core of our practice. As a firm, we are dedicated to the future.

The NBBJ Partners

Introduction

NBBJ—Designing Common Ground

By Erika Rosenfeld, PhD

"Every culture requires some avenue for addressing and thereby explicating its identities, accomplishments, and needs."[1]

NBBJ is not quite like any other architecture practice. It has a staff of 600 and projects—as many as 900 at any one time—all over the world, but it doesn't "feel" large or global. It practices in 19 studios, spread among six offices in the US, but it is not diffuse or disconnected. It has a strong, coherent identity and mission, but gives its staff extraordinary autonomy and freedom. No building or interior designed by NBBJ reflects a single, firm-defining style, but every project is informed by the same set of complex, deeply held principles. Its leadership is rigorously businesslike and architecturally visionary, as committed to serving its clients and society as it is to producing exceptional design.

If NBBJ sounds utterly paradoxical, it is—by design.

"Design," of course, is what architects do: they design buildings, interiors, places. But an examination of the word's multiple meanings—conceive, invent, plan, draw, create, compose, intend—reveals a rich, even contradictory, texture: the notion of design becomes an interestingly paradoxical marriage of intuition and reason, imagination and logic, words and images. Such texture and paradox are at the heart of NBBJ, informing not only its *raison d'être*, but the practice itself. NBBJ has designed itself as a firm, designs the process by which it sees projects through, designs each relationship with a client.

Today, NBBJ is a major player in the global business of architecture. It is the sixth largest architecture firm in the world—the second largest in the US—with projects throughout North America, the Far East, Europe, and South America. There are few, if any, building types it has not designed.

It is also well on its way to being a significant shape-giver to the art of architecture, and here, too, the firm's approach is complex and unusual. In firms of NBBJ's size and reach, design excellence is often sacrificed to the care and feeding of the organizational machine. Others are known for a signature style, issuing in sketch form from the imagination of a single designer and identifiable in every project.

NBBJ has instead embraced a firm-wide allegiance to exceptional design that emerges from and is created for the people, culture, and ethos of a particular place—design for "context" in its greatest complexity and sophistication. In that view, architecture is necessarily an integrated physical response to a diverse set of values and needs. Good architecture is emphatically of its time and of its place, balancing economic benefit, environmental asset, and enduring experiential delight. No single, underlying design characteristic marks NBBJ's projects as the work of one hand, nor are they driven solely by academic theory. Rather, the firm has adopted a form of regionalism as the common denominator, the prism through which the primary design influences— program, site, climate, and historical and architectural

[1] Thomas B. Farrell, *Norms of Rhetorical Culture.* Yale University Press, 1993, p. 9.

precedents, among others—are refracted. Given the variety of its projects and clients, of the locations in which it works, even of its own partners and staff, discovering and giving form to that concept presents NBBJ with its most challenging task: the design of common ground, within the firm itself and where client, society, environment, and the architect's vision meet.

If NBBJ arrived at its present eminence and philosophy by design, its beginnings and early years followed a less deliberate path. But the circumstances of its founding and growth, the character of its leadership, and the radical changes of the marketplace in recent decades combined to give NBBJ its singular identity and strengths.

Designing NBBJ

In 1943, Seattle architects Floyd Naramore, William Bain, Clifton Brady, and Perry Johanson banded together to take on a number of war-time projects. At the war's end, they formalized their relationship, practicing as Naramore, Bain, Brady, and Johanson—hence NBBJ—and were responsible for major projects in their home town throughout the ensuing three decades. By the mid-1970s, the firm had expanded considerably in size and range, successfully pursuing work well beyond its regional base.

When, in 1976, NBBJ received the commission to design a major project more than 2,000 miles away in Columbus, Ohio, the firm's partners entered into a collaboration with the Columbus-based firm of Nitschke-Godwin-Böhm to undertake the project. A year and many probing conversations later, the two firms merged, eventually becoming NBBJ.

This development initiated what was to become a pattern for NBBJ's growth over the following decade, as it sought and won opportunities for work farther and farther afield. Within a relatively short time, NBBJ had multiple offices and a variety of relationships with other practices. No longer a Seattle- and Columbus-based firm, it was truly national.

In the early 1980s, NBBJ entered a period of re-evaluation, reaffirming its core values and committing to an ambitious mission: to be "the best design firm." From an intense process of analysis and strategic planning there emerged a new structure, modus operandi, and, gradually, a clearly articulated design approach which responded in equal measure to the firm's character and ethos and to the realities of contemporary architectural practice.

Several factors converged to influence these decisions. NBBJ had by then a long history of socially and environmentally responsible design, combined with a commitment to client service based as much in a principle of ethical practice as in that of good business. At the same time, the growing number and variety of its commissions made NBBJ increasingly attractive to exceptionally talented architects, leading inevitably to the setting of higher standards of design as well as a broader range of specialization. And NBBJ recognized that the continuing satisfaction of its bright young staff demanded opportunities to expand their skills, advance within the firm, and make a contribution to the field of architecture.

The firm's leadership was aware, too, that, as business, political, and social boundaries blurred across the globe, a countering force was gaining strength: one that seeks the enhancement and protection of regional characteristics and cultural identity. NBBJ itself mirrored these opposing trends: it was a large firm, practicing globally from offices in locations with a strong sense of regional personality and pride.

In redesigning NBBJ, the partners sought not to alter the fundamental principles, character, and strengths of the firm, but to create structures and practices to sustain them. They began by reorganizing NBBJ as a firm with two foci: the Eastern region, administered from Columbus and responsible for offices in New York City and North Carolina; and the Western region, administered from Seattle and comprising additional offices in San Francisco and Los Angeles. The firm was further subdivided into studios, of no more than 35 people each, which in turn furnished teams for individual projects.

The resulting structure responds to more than just the need to manage efficiently a large and far-flung organization; it is, as NBBJ's partners conceive it, a vehicle designed expressly to enable the complex processes by which the firm's paradoxes are held in dynamic balance.

Designing Studios

These processes are reflected in the make-up and practices of NBBJ's studios—in effect a collection of medium-sized firms operating in a supporting matrix that only a very large firm can provide. Each group is small enough to ensure that all members are fully aware of the status of their studio's projects, but large enough to provide a complete balance of skills. Though studio members may have different talents and experience, collectively they are the "complete architect." Notwithstanding their individual strengths and responsibilities, each is expected to be adept in every aspect of architecture as NBBJ practices it: the design of communication with clients; of the functional requirement of various building types; of the process for managing a project; of systems and aesthetics. Studio leadership is similarly balanced—by a triumvirate: the process designer, who is the operations lead; what the firm calls the "spiritual" designer, responsible for keeping faith with the project's vision; and the building systems designer, or technical lead.

A second, more fluid organizational pattern, cutting across studio and geographic lines, brings together ad hoc groups of principals to address such issues as practice, operations, marketing, special initiatives, and strategy. Weaving the whole NBBJ fabric together are the partners, who serve as leaders, teachers, and mentors, ensuring that a coherent and consistent ethos permeates the firm and that the next generation is nurtured and encouraged.

Most unusually for a large firm, NBBJ assembles the entire project team from the start and keeps it intact throughout the process, ensuring the balanced and continuous involvement of people with multiple skills. This approach provides for a diversity of perspectives that enhances the potential for true innovation.

More critically, perhaps, because all the participants hear first-hand what the client has to say and see the client's reactions for themselves, communication with the client and within the team is greatly facilitated, saving time and eliminating second-guessing as the project moves forward.

The size and structure of the studio also hold individual initiative and team effort in careful balance. NBBJ gives its staff considerable latitude to exercise their own judgment, and, with this, equally great responsibility for and sense of ownership of their projects. Even on a fast-track job, a studio may begin with a day-long discussion of individual styles of communication and differences of approach, in effect designing an approach to the project that invests each member in its outcome and ensures a common ground within the studio and with the client.

Designing Balance and Diversity

There is a further purpose to the studio system and to the firm's operational style that goes to the heart of NBBJ's culture: seeking balance in diversity. This is nowhere more evident than among the nine partners, whose backgrounds, education, age, and personalities are enormously varied. Differences of perspective, cultural assumptions, and skills are not merely accepted, they are actively sought and cultivated.

Throughout NBBJ, a similarly compatible diversity has been shaped by the continuous design of common ground. Not surprisingly, the design process is essentially narrative: a community, after all, is a group of people who know the same stories. The creation and nurturing of community involves discovering common myths, themes, and metaphors and collaborating on the design of new ones.

NBBJ's architects spend much time listening, talking, and writing to one another. Because the firm is collegial, its consensus-driven decisions made by staff rather than handed down by fiat of the partners, constant and open communication at all levels is essential to its culture. Although much of this activity is concerned with the minutiae of running a complex company, even more is devoted to exploring and articulating differences and similarities of belief and ideas, whether about organization, management, or architecture itself. NBBJ actively fosters intellectual inquiry—its architects are uncommonly well read across a wide range of disciplines, and the firm's Oregano program sends groups of younger designers to study and explore architecture overseas—as well as the sharing of learning and discovery.

Over the years in which the process of designing the firm was at its most intense, members of NBBJ met frequently and in various configurations, not only to discuss, refine, and promulgate decisions, but to establish common storylines. Each studio—comprised of local natives and "transplants" from other regions and NBBJ offices—in turn makes the firm-wide narrative its own, adding the color and detail of its members' personalities and educational and practical experience. The result is a constancy of basic themes, retold with great variety of detail and imagery in the local language and culture.

At the same time, such on-going discussion helps mitigate two potential drawbacks of NBBJ's structure: competition and fragmentation. Inevitably, studios—"owning" their projects as they do—develop a sense of competitiveness; and the close working environment of each studio leads to the development of a culture that, in isolation, may diverge from the firm-wide ethos. But the ongoing conversations, particularly within the mentor groups made up of studio leaders, ensure the sharing of insights and learning, airing of professional issues, and cultivation of common ground and mutual support. Moreover, the firm's absolute insistence on individual responsibility extends from that individual's immediate assignment to the entire practice: collaboration is necessitated by the over-riding rule that, simply put, "no one wins unless everyone wins."

Just as the process of sustaining such balance is ongoing, complex, and thoughtful, so is NBBJ's approach to its work—to the design of client relations, process, and project—which requires in equal measure the practical, psychological, cultural, and visionary.

Designing Communication

In NBBJ's culture, achievement is measured not by a design's conceptual excellence, but by its realization, the keys to which— funds, timing, will, and interpersonal relations—are held by the client. Thus it should come as no surprise that, especially on complex projects, NBBJ designates a "communications designer," charged with ensuring that the client both is and feels well served.

To a large extent, NBBJ's client relations are based in its own business acumen, combined with an extensive and continually renewed understanding of the markets it serves and the forces that act on them. The firm's sports facilities experts have as firm a grasp of the economics of team ownership and operations as they do of stadium design; the commercial building specialists are conversant in financing; the health care designers envision the future of medical practice. Quite apart from establishing a community of knowledge with clients, such expertise also enables the firm to make good on its commitment to provide whatever a client may need, even when that extends well beyond traditional services.

With respect to individual clients, however, NBBJ approaches each relationship without preconceptions, taking pains to understand the values, concerns, objectives, even fears that motivate each member of the client team. The relationship and the process that sustains it throughout a project are designed, through exploratory sessions, informal discussion, and consensus-building, to reflect and support the client's issues and personality. The consequent clarity and openness of communication about every aspect of a project help establish a common ground of expectation, both in the process and its outcome.

What NBBJ calls its "culture of partnership" with clients involves the design of the business relationship as well. In order to ensure that the firm's ethos is truly all-pervasive, the administrative functions are also organized into a studio, with the same internal structure and design-based processes as the other studios, who are its clients. Administrators, too, are responsible for and vested in each project's success, designing their procedures and documentation to each client's specific practices and needs.

If this requires uncommon flexibility, it also results in unusually comfortable client relations and significant efficiencies.

Efficiency is not an objective customarily associated with design excellence. For NBBJ, however, the design of management methods and a supporting organization that create great efficiencies is essential to sustain what for many firms would be a prohibitively costly approach to design. That approach rests on the assumption that serving clients, society, the environment, and the art of architecture calls for full and open-minded participation in the client's goals, sensitive and thorough definition of issues, and the development of alternatives not bound by existing paradigms.

Once again, the key lies in balance—in this case, of control and rigor with freedom and creativity. At the beginning of each project phase, the entire studio meets to develop a strategy for that phase and to establish project benchmarks that are revisited in weekly tactical meetings. The strategy responds to questions about where design dollars can and should be spent, how functional requirements can best be satisfied, where value can be added through exceptional design. By determining which elements can truly benefit from exhaustive design exploration and which are better served by more standard approaches, where energy should be focused, and how to help the client make decisions necessary to advance the project, NBBJ is able not only to take on projects whose restrictive budget and tight schedule others might find daunting, but also to make of them some of its greatest successes.

Designing Architecture

Balance is also the principle that holds in creative tension the paradoxes inherent in the definition of design that NBBJ so enthusiastically embraces. The creation of multiple, often unexpected alternatives requires an environment that enables the participation of diverse minds, logical and intuitive, and of multiple skills. Insisting on the early and continuous involvement not only of the project team and client, but of engineers, estimators, builders, and others, the firm encourages rigorous questioning and challenge. Exposure to a diversity of skills, talents, and intelligences helps the architects resist the impulse to accept the first solution that presents itself. The firm's culture invites individuals to contribute to issues outside their expertise and places a high value on the different perspectives and approaches to problem-solving that are born of varying experience and ways of thinking.

As they are applied to the design of buildings and interiors themselves, NBBJ's principles and practices are equally complex. And as it does internally and with its clients, the firm also seeks to identify and design a common ground with the components of a regional narrative, located through exhaustive research, investigation, experience, reflection, and analysis.

This emphasis on region and community speaks importantly to an essential of NBBJ's design ethic: that its work is created for a cultural and social setting in which judgment is passed by, and welcomed from, the client, the users, passersby. The meaning found in a building by people who experience it daily is a function of its reflection and enhancement of regional values.

Context is always a challenge. NBBJ has chosen to make context, in its broadest and richest sense, an inspiration. Seeking the elements of invention from the regional characteristics of the places in which it works, the firm goes well beyond issues of local aesthetics, geography, climate, or materials, to include components of what might be called the "personality" of a region and its people. The firm explores the culture and ethos of a place, the myths as well as the realities that comprise the narrative community. History—local, architectural, even personal—is woven together with characteristics that reveal important clues about relationships: formality or informality, accessibility or exclusivity, community and privacy.

The process of discovery is painstaking. Even when the firm practices on one of its home grounds, it goes to extraordinary lengths to avoid preconceptions, challenge its own assumptions, and look with a fresh and inquisitive eye at its surroundings. But the value of such exploration reveals itself even more plainly when NBBJ leaves its own communities to practice in other cultures, where even the most obvious local attribute—color or material or motif—may have important embedded meaning. Taking nothing for granted, the firm makes of each project a search for an appropriate regional architectural language that has consistent, predictable communal meaning, through which to tell a story that is at once familiar and new and, above all, respectful of the regional ethos.

Story-telling is enjoying a resurgence of popularity, not only in literature, but in the law, medicine, and in all the arts, including architecture. Narrative, it seems, is necessary: it is the fundamental unit of knowledge, the foundation of memory, the way in which people make sense of their lives. Since story-telling is essentially a communal activity, it is also, significantly, the way in which groups—whether family, firm, or region—make and renew their bonds.

Such continual making and renewing is the engine that motivates NBBJ. It is not accidental that the word "designing," like "story-telling," suggests continuity and process. NBBJ is determined always to be in a state of becoming. It resists stasis strenuously and with all its resources, looking constantly for ways to test itself, to put an edge on its work and its practice.

NBBJ makes architecture the way story-tellers have always made narratives: by collecting images, themes, values, ideas, and metaphors and then, with artistry and craft, designing a work that unites and enriches a community. The best of the firm's work does just that: it engenders in those for whom it was made strong feelings of possessiveness and affection for a place they recognize as their common ground.

Erika Rosenfeld is a New York-based writer who specializes in architecture and related fields.

COMMERCE

Corregidor-Bataan Memorial

Design 1957
Corregidor Island, The Phillipines
World War II Pacific Theater War Memorial Commission
Winning competition entry

This was the winning entry in an international competition to memorialize World War II in the Pacific. The project was constructed many years later under the constraints of a sharply reduced budget, so the design illustrated here was never realized.

1

2

1   Perspective and plan views
2   View from the harbor

1001 Fourth Avenue

Design/Completion 1968/1970
Seattle, Washington
Seattle-First National Bank
50 stories: 1 million gross square feet (650,000 square feet office,
7,000 square feet retail, and 800-car parking)
Steel
Bronze anodized aluminum

For many years Seattle's tallest building, this 50-story tower was designed to accommodate the headquarters of Seattle-First National Bank (Seafirst) and a substantial number of tenant offices.

The tower is supported by four massive steel corner columns and a central elevator core. Each exterior wall consists of Verendeel steel trusses for optimum efficiency and economy. The truss system transfers vertical, seismic, and wind loads to tapered corner piers at each floor, which graduate in size as the load increases. This configuration eliminates the need for interior supports and frees the floor plan for maximum size and efficiency.

Sheathed in bronze anodized aluminum, the building towered for years above all others on the Seattle skyline, and earned praise from critics such as Ada Louise Huxtable.

1

1   East façade, looking towards the harbor

Sitka Indian Village Redevelopment Plan

Design/Completion 1972/1974
Sitka, Alaska
Sitka Village Planning Council

By the early 1970s, the Sitka Indian Village on the southeast coast of Alaska had become a dilapidated enclave on a stretch of prime waterfront, its people refusing traditional notions of urban renewal that sought to relocate them to public housing projects.

Though tribal income precluded private sector mortgages, the Village Planning Council convinced the Sitka Borough Assembly to ameliorate the decline, which included substandard housing and inadequate water and sewer services. The Borough responded, and matching funds were granted from state and federal agencies on the condition that a comprehensive plan be devised.

NBBJ sent a planner and his family to live in the village for five months. A provisional plan was completed with the active participation of the naturally reserved Tlingit community. The subsequent redevelopment project preserved historic clan houses, stabilized the village, forestalled relocation, and prevented outside speculative development.

1

2

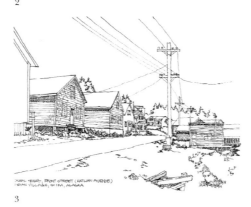

3

4

0 50 100ft

1&2 Existing village
3 Sketch of existing village
4 Plan of village

United States Pavilion, Expo '74

Design/Completion 1973/1974
Spokane, Washington
US Department of Commerce, General Services Administration
180,000 square feet
Fiberglass fabric over stressed cable; earth berms

Designed as a temporary structure for the 1974 World Exposition, the United States Pavilion proved so popular with Spokane citizens that it remains standing today, a permanent fixture on the Spokane skyline.

Covered with Teflon-coated translucent fiberglass fabric, the pavilion exhibit area comprised the center third of the US Pavilion Complex, with a permanent Federal Action Center to the west and an 850-seat I-Max theater to the east.

The off-white soft-shell roof spans 320 feet over a network of stressed cables, forming a hyperboloid of revolution around a leaning mast.

Because of planning delays, NBBJ was selected to design the pavilion just three months before construction was scheduled to begin. The firm responded with a design concept in three weeks and the pavilion, subsequently featured on the cover of *Progressive Architecture* magazine, opened on time.

1

2

1 Trussed support mast
2 View from the river

Honolulu Municipal Office Building

Design/Completion 1970/1975
Honolulu, Hawaii
City and County of Honolulu
17 stories: 450,000 gross square feet/385,000 net square feet
Exposed reinforced concrete
Glass
Winning competition entry

Constructed of reinforced concrete, the Honolulu Municipal Office Building steps outward to each side, with floors 66 feet wide at the second story and 88 feet wide at the fifteenth. As the building rises to broader floors it requires less support, providing a progressively larger duct area as the solid portion of each column gradually diminishes towards the top. Air from the rooftop mechanical system enters this space and is distributed laterally to each floor through hollow girders.

The corner column design insures a column-free interior office plan that provides a clear span of at least 117 feet at each floor for maximum flexibility. The design also greatly diminishes solar loading: as each floor extends 18 inches beyond the floor below it, windows are shaded from the tropical sun, yet still take in sweeping views of the surrounding mountains and ocean.

The Municipal Building stands near the Hawaii State Capitol Building and the historic Iolani Palace.

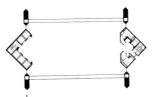

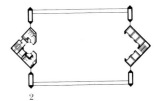

1

2

3

1   Plan at second story
2   Plan at thirteenth story
3   View from the Capital grounds

Merrill Place, Adaptive Reuse, Restoration and Additions

Design/Completion 1982/1984
Seattle, Washington
Heritage Group, Inc.
7 stories: 61,000 square feet
Heavy timber with steel columns
Brick veneer skin

This redevelopment project in Seattle's historic Pioneer Square district presented a unique opportunity to reopen the history book and add a dramatic new chapter. Combining historic restoration with new construction, the adaptive reuse project reclaimed a block of aging office buildings as a mixed-use complex to create an urban environment in which living, leisure, and work co-exist harmoniously and provide a strong anchor to neighborhood revitalization.

As the façades of the main building were required to be restored by historic ordinances, one of the smaller structures was cut away on the interior of the block and re-skinned with a tiered glass curtain wall that infuses the complex with natural light and opens onto a courtyard with reflective pool and waterfall. The courtyard revitalizes the site, providing a rich contrast between old and new, and drawing passersby through the alley to discover a surprising garden area in the midst of downtown. The trees and the sound of falling water dampen the noise from an adjacent elevated roadway.

1

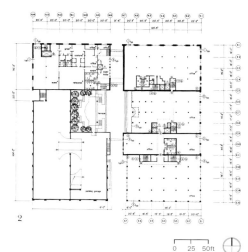

2

0 25 50ft

3

1   View from the courtyard looking east
2   Plan view
3   View from the garage looking northeast

Four Seasons Olympic Hotel, Renovation and Restoration

Design/Completion 1979/1981
Seattle, Washington
Urban Investment and Development Company/Four Seasons Hotels Ltd
506,000 square feet
Exterior masonry walls reinforced with steel studs
Terra cotta; glass-reinforced concrete castings and finishes

Built in the Italian Renaissance style by architect George B. Post & Sons in 1924, the Olympic Hotel was always a haven of cultured elegance in the frontier wilds of the Pacific Northwest, and is now listed on the National Register of Historic Places.

As part of the renovation, the hotel's intricate terra cotta trim was painstakingly cleaned, and damaged pieces repaired with glass-reinforced concrete castings and finishes matched to the originals. Much of the cast-iron was recast and replaced. Where pieces of the fascia had been demolished by earlier additions, new molds based on original shop drawings were designed and new pieces cast.

The most dramatic and visible exterior improvement was the removal of an enclosed motor entry and ballroom addition from the 1950s and the construction of a new entrance. Other additions included a glass-enclosed pool house and health club over the south lobby.

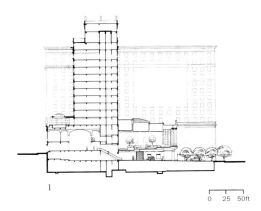

1

0   25   50ft

2

1   North–south section through entry court
2   New entry court
3   New pool and spa
4   Dining room entry from lobby
5   New pool above former main entry

24

3

4

5

The Heritage Building Restoration and Adaptive Reuse

Design 1982
Seattle, Washington
South Jackson Street Associates
5 stories: 72,000 square feet
Wood frame with sandstone and brick

The meticulously restored façade gives little hint of the comprehensive interior reconstruction that transformed this 1904 landmark warehouse, listed on the National Register of Historic Places, into the western headquarters of NBBJ.

Structural and mechanical improvements included seismic upgrading, new plywood diaphragms for each floor, steel beam supports at each column, new relocated stairs and elevators, indirect lighting, and air conditioning.

While the brick load-bearing walls and heavy timber structure were cleaned and left exposed, the building's five floors, basement, and roof were refitted to serve NBBJ's studio system. A custom partition system establishes a highly flexible modern work environment in the midst of the preserved historic shell.

Continued

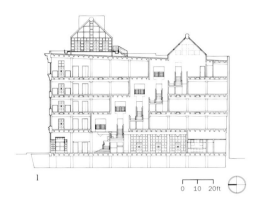

1

0 10 20ft

2

1   North–south section through new central stair
2   North façade
3   New central stair from entrance lobby

3

A switchbacked central stair climbs through the building, weaving in and out of one of its enclosing walls and culminating in a giant skylight. Reminiscent of an Italian hilltown streetscape, balcony-like portals overlook the stairs and encourage impromptu greeting and conversation.

A glazed greenhouse-style belvedere that opens onto a landscaped deck offers an all-purpose, sunlit getaway from the offices below, providing a rooftop lunch and meeting area as well as a starlit pavilion for receptions and parties. With neither cooling nor heating, the year-round pavilion offers shelter from Seattle's winter rains while admitting light and warmth and preserving a panoramic view of downtown Seattle, Elliott Bay, and the distant Olympic Mountains.

4

5

6

4   Lobby looking east
5&6 Rooftop pavilion
7   Balcony overlooking central stair
8   Fourth floor plan
9   First floor plan
10 View from central stair looking east

7

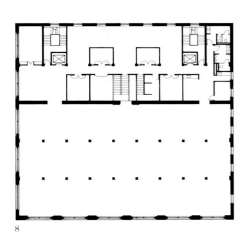

8

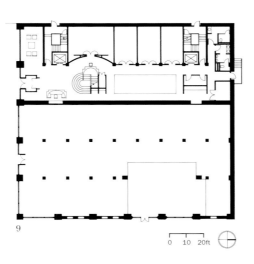

9

0 10 20ft

10

Market Place Tower

Design/Completion 1987/1988
Seattle, Washington
The Koll Company (Koll Development Real Estate Group)
17 stories mixed use: 193,099 square feet retail and office,
35,000 square feet residential, 200-car parking
Structural steel frame over four-story concrete parking structure
Green Burlington slate base with white marble accents; windows
in aggregate granite grid

The greenhouse-like elements of high-end condominiums climb against the Seattle skyline filling a zoning "envelope" and recalling the steep and often densely packed hills of Seattle's residential neighborhoods. Commercial offices, retail at street level, and parking in the steeply sloping base are the other components of this mixed-use mid-rise.

Office and residential users have separate entrances of appropriately different character. Individual stainless steel mailbox covers etched with the markings of canceled stamps and bearing the names of each condominium owner are individually lit above cantilevered glass shelves in the residential lobby. Opposite, a fireplace—the quintessential Northwest symbol of hospitality—welcomes visitors and offers a pleasant area for waiting.

Cast glass screens in the office lobby suggest Seattle's watery environment and refer to its reputation as one of the world's great centers of glass art.

1

1   East façade with office and residential entrances
2   Typical office level plan
3   Typical condominium level plan
4   Office lobby with glass screen
5   View from condominium
6   Residential lobby with individual mailboxes

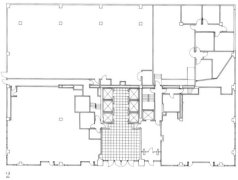

2

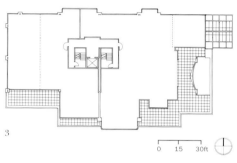

3

0　15　30ft

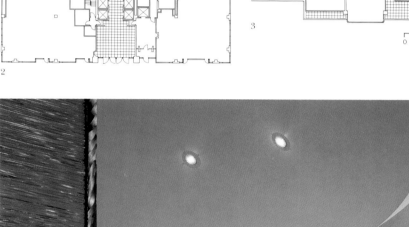

5

4

6

Two Union Square

Design/Completion 1985/1989
Seattle, Washington
Unico Properties, Inc. with Metropolitan Life Insurance Co.
& Security Pacific Bancorp
1,206,300 gross square feet (910,000 net square feet office;
45,000 net square feet retail and gardens; 1000-car garage)
Steel-braced frame with concrete-filled steel pipe columns
Reflective glass curtain wall with white metal spandrels

*"A step forward in high-rise design. Poetic,
lyric, and responsive to the urban setting.
It is one of the best high-rises, both nationally
and internationally, in the past few years."*
Peter Pran, AIA Honor Awards Juror

Unlike anything previously built, Two
Union Square embodies new design
concepts, new building materials, and
new construction techniques in the most
advanced application of a highly ductile
composite column system.

Rising from a sparkling three-tiered retail
plaza in the heart of downtown Seattle,
2U2 (as it is noted in shorthand)
celebrates several firsts: the first tower
to utilize steel pipes filled with a concrete
stronger than any used commercially
before (at 19k psi, a 35 percent increase
for a new world record); the first to
employ uniquely efficient viscoelastic
dampers and belt-truss framing to control
building movement; the first to provide

Continued

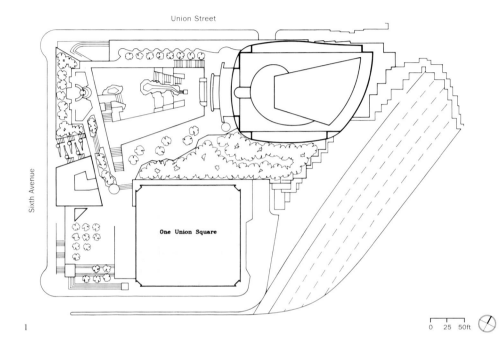

1 Site plan
2 Two Union Square at the heart of
   downtown Seattle
3 Main lobby, third floor, details

unequaled exterior column spacing of as much as 46 feet (contrasting the conventional 15 to 20 feet) thus allowing each floor as many as 10 cantilevered corner offices with continuous wraparound windows. Admirable accomplishments alone, these technical feats also increased performance, shortened construction time (structural floors of 23,000 square feet were completed at a rate of one every 10 working hours), and reduced estimated structural costs by $10 million.

Its unprecedented footprint of soft curvilinear forms complements its older companion, One Union Square, by recalling established themes and proportions while presenting an inspired reinterpretation of both its immediate urban context and the Pacific Northwest region.

A flowing wave form provides a guiding design motif that unexpectedly reveals and rhythmically repeats itself throughout the building. Sometimes suggesting a sail or prow or the aerodynamic plane of a metallic wing, the form insistently evokes

Continued

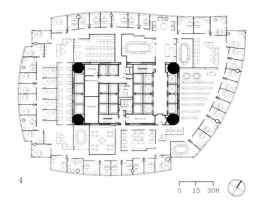

4

5

4   Typical office floor plan
5   Courtyard with wave-form benches; details from
    earlier building on this site
6   Geometric construction of wave-form benches
7   One of two adjacent entry markers illustrating
    plans of One and Two Union Square towers
8   Northwest images and related design
    manifestations

6

7

8

Seattle's culture of jets, hydrofoils, ships, and sailboats, as well as the region's defining elemental forces of wind and water.

Drawing inspiration from Seattle's history as a maritime and aerospace port and as a forest-rich, mountain-nestled lumber town, NBBJ architects modeled the tower's external shape and internal appointments on the landscape—city and region—that it reflects and helps organize as one of the city's tallest buildings. Thus, 2U2 becomes an icon of the values, natural environment, and economic resources of the Northwest.

At ground level, entry steps represent ocean surf leading into a lobby beach of ocean-spray carpet custom-designed with a patterning of rippled sand. Elevator corridors evoke the magnificent Northwest forests with Makore wood and Baltic Brown granite panels, moss green doors and carpets, and dappled light. High above, the tower peaks with the snow-white cap of a streamlined penthouse that evokes

Continued

9

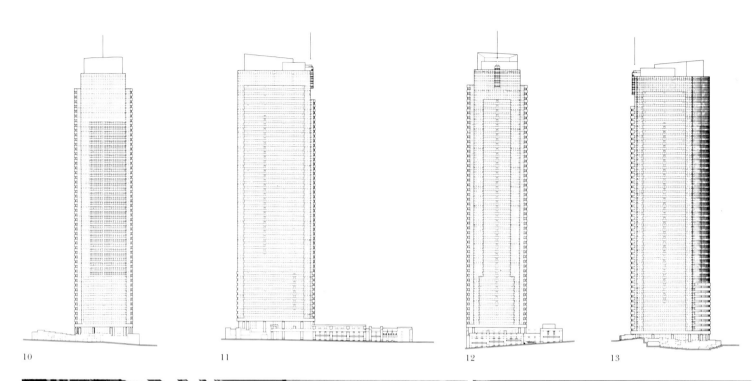

10

11

12

13

14

both the surrounding mountains and the fin of a racing hydroplane—thus suggesting both the natural and technological riches of the region.

Brilliant white horizontal spandrels on 2U2 relate to the façade of the more stout One Union without overpowering it, rather playing on the towers' relationship by visually reversing the latter's horizontal patterning. Slightly inset from the corners, these bands also lend the larger building a more slender carriage than its great width might otherwise present, and at the same time suggest the striped bark of indigenous cedar trees, the full sails of merchant clipper ships that established Seattle, and the aerodynamism of airfoils and jet wings that guide the city's future.

Similarly, materials vary as the building rises, from a solid granite base with flame-finish adding texture at eye level, to polished stone at lobby level, to the unadorned metal-and-glass upper stories reaching to the white-cap peak.

Continued

15

16

15   Forest-like elevator lobby with dappled light
16   Courtyard entrance from west with ramp for handicapped
17   Exterior walkway; north side at lobby level

17

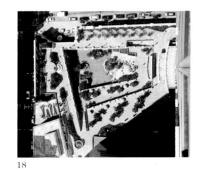

18

These subtle metaphors distinguish the building's four faces as well, their curvatures deriving from a series of interlocking circles and echoing the neighborhood approaching a given side.

This satisfying aesthetic response to the surrounding environment derives from the structural strategy of placing all wind- and earthquake-resisting elements within interior core walls—which increased space planning efficiency by 10 percent and assured open office space that fully enjoys the tower's splendid-in-all-directions vistas.

The tower's quartet of 10-foot-diameter interior columns comprised 5/8-inch steel pipes filled with the strongest concrete ever used in a commercial structure. Nearly four times stronger than conventional concrete, yet far less costly than steel framing, this innovative material allows the building's primary load to rest on the four interior columns with 14 smaller support columns at the perimeter. The result is an exceptionally marketable
Continued

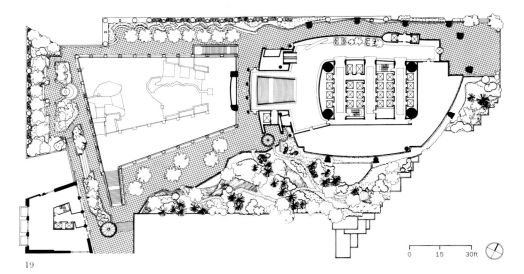

0   15   30ft

19

20

18 Courtyard as seen from the building's twentieth floor
19 Third floor plan
20 Courtyard panorama
21 Exterior from below

floorplan assuring numerous structurally free corner offices—an average of 10 per floor.

2U2 assumes an integral place in the city with a full acre of public open-air courtyard. This block-long landscaped plaza with terraced walkways comprises half the site, and at ground level organizes restaurants and shops. Sited for maximum exposure to midday sun throughout the year, the open area brings fountains, stepped boulders, a creek and waterfall, and regional flora into an inviting urban context, and establishes a powerful focal point for Seattle community and culture.

As such, 2U2 stands as not merely a reflection of but a focal point for Seattle and the Northwest region.

22

23

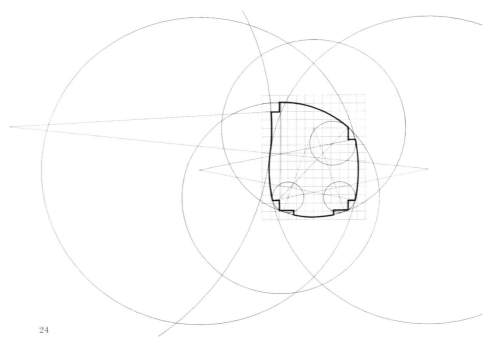
24

22   View from the west
23   View from the east
24   A geometric construction of the tower plan
25   North elevation with vertical lines keyed to adjacent streets

25

Sun Mountain Resort

Design/Completion 1987/1988 (Phase I), 1987/1991 (Phase II)
Winthrop, Washington
Sun Mountain Resorts, Inc./Village Resorts, Inc.
Two buildings in phased renovation and expansion
Exposed wooden beams

With exposed wooden beams, stone fireplaces, and handmade quilts evoking grand turn-of-the-century and Depression-era WPA lodges, Sun Mountain's design respects both the massive scale of the surrounding North Cascade Wilderness Area and the elegant simplicity of the local culture. The goal of upgrading the 30-year-old lodge and bringing it to four-star status was achieved through close attention to detail and careful responsiveness to setting and local resources.

The original Sun Mountain Lodge was built in 1962 (by Northwest architect Roland Terry) and consisted of a small lodge with separate guest room buildings. The first phase rebuilt these original structures while the second phase added a larger lodge building with guest rooms.

Continued

1

0   20   40ft

2

1 First floor plan of main lodge
2 New west façade of main lodge
3 Library fireplace detail
4 Plan of guest room building showing new
  bathrooms and entrance decks
5 Library
6 Main lodge from guest room building

3

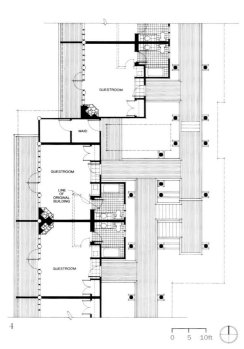

4

0   5   10ft

5

6

The lodge's remodeling and expansion responded to the culture, climate, and natural environment of the area by involving local artisans in building and furnishing the resort, located near Winthrop, a town that bustled with gold mining in the 1890s. Rusted iron fixtures, carved fireplace mantles, split log bar and registration counters, handcrafted furnishings, and carved details were the result of a collaboration between architect and artists. The lodge has now become a showplace for regional arts and crafts.

7

7   Typical guest room
8   New main lobby

State of Arizona Department of Administration Office Building

Design/Completion 1989/1992
Tucson, Arizona
State of Arizona, Department of Administration
144,000 square feet
Red brick veneer with steel-framed atrium

Arizona's DOA Office Building, which joins an existing office building with a large open atrium between, completes the development of this state property in downtown Tucson.

A curved north wall of patterned brick sweeps away from the basic rectilinear form of the building to follow the curve of a major urban arterial and to maximize floor space. The large floor plate of 27,000 square feet provides great flexibility for future reconfiguration, while a 9,000-square-foot steel-frame and aluminum atrium links the new north building with its southerly companion and establishes the primary orientation of the complex. While shading the building's south-facing windows, the open air, solar-screened atrium preserves southern vistas and provides garden-like views of its own.

Continued

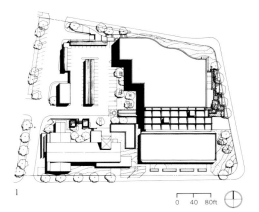

1

0 40 80ft

2

3

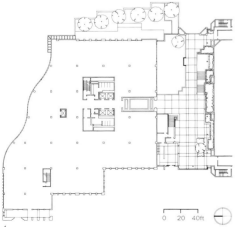

4

0   20   40ft

From the atrium visitors can move north into the new State Office Building lobby, south into the earlier State Office Building, up the stairway to the second-floor meeting room, or down the stairway to the cafeteria.

The DOA Office Building renews the traditional red brick detailing of the existing State Office Building on its northern side in a spontaneous signature pattern: red bricks interweave with cream bricks that suggest the sandy hue of a nearby complex. East and west façades use bricks identical in shape and color to those of the existing building.

5

5   Detail of curved window wall
6   Lobby connecting new building to atrium

6

Seattle-Tacoma International Airport
Concourse Improvements

Design/Completion 1991/1993
Seattle, Washington
Port of Seattle
455,000 gross square feet (156,000 gross square feet new construction)
Renovating appearance of and widening existing 30-gate Concourses B–D; adding seven new gates to Concourse D

With its emergence as a key gateway between the Pacific Northwest and the Pacific Rim, Sea-Tac International Airport required expansion in the early 1990s to meet burgeoning growth.

The new additions create distinct pavilions along each concourse to mitigate their apparent length, while widening them and increasing ceiling heights. Between 12 and 38 feet of width were added to various sections of each concourse to improve pedestrian traffic and allow larger concession areas, additional exits, and enlarged hold and VIP rooms. More than 30 gates were replaced, and Concourse D was extended by 400 feet to accommodate seven new gates. This distinctly white and bright airside identity contrasts sharply with the dark bronze and glass landside identity of the main terminal.

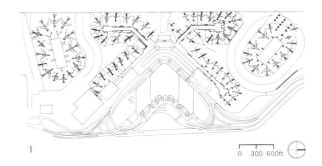

1

0 300 600ft

2

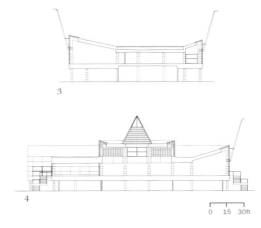

3

4

0 15 30ft

5

1 Plan showing concourse modifications
2 Airside view of Concourse D addition
3 Typical concourse section showing additions on both sides
4 Section through Concourse D addition
5 Concourse C alterations with sculpture by Nori Sato
6 Concourse D addition
7 Interior view showing transparent and translucent wall and ceiling panels
8 Translucent panels become opaque from exterior during daytime

6

7

8

United States Navy Family Support Complex

Design/Completion 1991/1995
Snohomish County, Washington
United States Navy
256,000 square feet on 52 acres
Brick; masonry; preformed metal panel; standing seam zinc/
aluminum roof; steel moment framed construction with a high
degree of glazing on clerestories and in atrium-type spaces;
translucent roof in chapel

The 52-acre Family Support Complex lies just north of Marysville, Washington, some 9 miles northeast of the Everett Navy Homeport it serves. The $37 million Smokey Point project was planned as a comprehensive village to accommodate short-term residential, recreational, and support needs. Each building was designed to announce its distinct character, identity, and function.

The campus organizing device is a large circle, segments of which are revealed at the entrances to the Base Exchange and the residential quarters, and in the landscape.

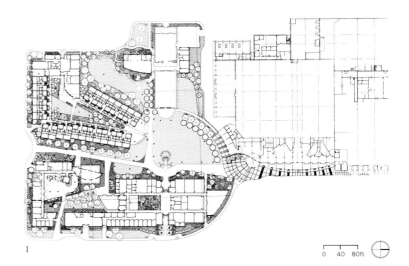

1

0   40   80ft

2

54

1 Site plan
2 Curving brick wall marks entrance to
  the Base Exchange
3 East elevation
4 Primary campus entrance

3

0 20 40ft

4

EDUCATIONAL SERVICES

5

6

7

5   Chapel entrance
6   Chapel courtyard
7   Campus as seen from the south entrance road
8   Interior view of chapel

West Lake Union Center

Design/Completion 1990/1994
Seattle, Washington
Fisher Properties, Inc.
10 stories: 380,000 square feet (including 22,000 square feet retail, 166,000 square feet parking)
Concrete and glass

Difficult yet attractive, the steeply sloping hillside proved to be the site's primary design consideration, not least because of a city ordinance limiting the building height to 65 feet to preserve an existing view corridor. The design represents a new generation office building that serves individuals working alone or in small groups, often using multiple computers.

The horseshoe-shaped West Lake Union Center cascades to the shores of Lake Union in stepped tiers that modulate the 380,000-square-foot building into varied office spaces, almost all with views of the lake. The building's shape and terracing also insure that an unusually high number of perimeter offices are accompanied by open areas, realized as interior balconies and exterior decks throughout the building.

Continued

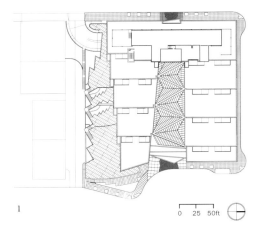

1

0   25   50ft

2

1 Site plan
2 Atrium
3 View from southeast
4 Typical floor plan
5 Terrace view looking east

3

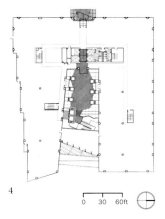

4

0 30 60ft

5

Origami, the Japanese art of folding paper, inspired the building's skylight of variously angled tetrahedrons that catch and reflect light, suggesting the appearance of water tumbling down the hill to the lake. The 8,500-square-foot court, finished with maple panels and granite column covers, establishes an open, airy community square with trees, interior balconies, and a steel-framed, glass-enclosed elevator.

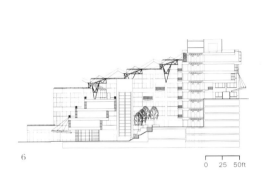

6

0   25   50ft

7

8

6   Section through atrium looking south
7   Atrium detail from above
8   Tenant lobby
9   Night view from the southeast

9

Global Gateway

Design/Completion 1995/1997
Changwon, Kyong Nam Province, South Korea
Samsung Corporation
165,000 square meters (1.7 million square feet)
Various materials in a mixed-use complex of five structures
Winning competition entry

"Let us open the door to our buildings, rooms, and ... that of our minds so that we can see the world."

Chairman Lee Kun-Hee's declaration of the Samsung Corporation's new management philosophy permeates this competition-winning design for a 1.7-million-square-foot mixed-use development. Embracing the guiding principles of synergy, unity, and humanity—as codified in Samsung's program of quality management, multifaceted integration, and globalization—Global Gateway celebrates the foundations of Korean ingenuity and industry while reaching out to the diverse influences and opportunities of the world.

The Global Gateway "pentad" of structures incorporates disparate programs: retail and office space; self-improvement (fitness, educational, and medical facilities); sports and leisure accommodations (such as Samsung's visionary Future Dream World and Windows to the World); convenience and hospitality (quality restaurants and hotels); and parking. Global Gateway integrates

Continued

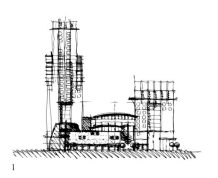

1

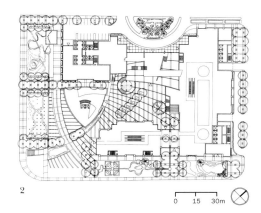

2

0   15   30m

3

1 Concept sketch
2 Site plan
3 View from the south
4 Courtyard view

4

these contrasting elements as complementary components of a seamless, unified environment that balances Korean tradition with technological expressions appropriate to the dawn of a new internationalist millennium.

Stone columns and beam frames define the lower levels and convey the strength and enduring spirit of Samsung and Korea. As the high- and mid-rise towers rise from this solid foundation, they assume a more open character with a glass and silvery metal façade that looks out to the surrounding mountains and the world beyond.

5

5   "Future Dream World" concept sketch
6   Model view from the south

Suyoung Bay Conceptual Master Plan

Design/Completion 1994/1999
Pusan, South Korea
Daewoo Corporation
1.4-million-square-meter (345-acre) mixed-use waterfront development
Second place competition entry

The object in this 10-block multi-use development plan was to establish a community rich in variety. The guiding planning principles included demonstration of Korea's central role in the emerging information, telecommunications, and electronics industries, and celebration of the rich cultural heritage of the gateway port of Pusan and the resort town of Haeundae ("place of sea and clouds").

Image and activity reinforce each other in a complex of memorable structures and engaging functions. Among the uses incorporated are multi-family residences, vacation hotels, office and retail, recreational and athletics facilities, entertainment and education complexes, an aquarium, and multi-use performance halls.

The office tower is envisioned as a shining beacon for the people of Korea, a landmark to their success as they voyage into the next millennium. As host to the 2002 Asian Games, the city of Pusan and Suyoung Bay have the potential to be a centerpiece of international activity.

1

2

1 View of office tower
2 Site model
3 Concept sketch
4 View of inner harbor

3

4

China Ocean Shipping Company Building

Design/Completion 1995/1998
Beijing, People's Republic of China
China Ocean Shipping Company (COSCO)
96,000 square meters (1,033,344 square feet)
Concrete frame, stone exterior
Winning competition entry

Combining historical Chinese massing with the sinuous lines of ocean freighters, this design won an international competition in 1994 for Cosco's new headquarters.

As a major competitor in international shipping, Cosco asked that its new facility reflect the sensibilities of its central Beijing location yet announce its global vision and role with a building embodying both modernity and aspiration for the future.

The 96,000-square-meter complex brings Cosco's 15,500 square meters of administrative core together with 56,910 square meters of retail and rental office space, and three levels of underground auto and bicycle parking.

The result is a headquarters building that honors Chinese precedents and recalls maritime commerce, incorporating these influences in a distinctly modern statement that expresses Cosco's bold vision of its future.

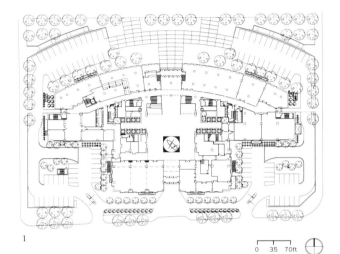

1

0   35   70ft

2

1   Site plan
2   South elevation
3   North elevation
4   Typical floor plan
5   East elevation

3

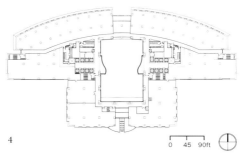

4

0 45 90ft

5

Fuxing Mansion

Design/Completion 1995/1997
South Bund, Shanghai, People's Republic of China
Shanghai Li Hua Real Estate Company
120,000 square meters (1.3 million square feet)
with 8-story podium and two 38-story towers
Concrete structural frame
Stone, glass, metal

Standing at the important intersection of Zhongshan and Fuxing roads, the connecting point between the developing South Bund district and Old Shanghai and the YuYuan Gardens, this mixed-use complex serves as a defining architectural nexus between the old and new centers of town.

The two towers collaborate in a single curving composition addressing the main corner of the site. The eastern tower presents to the Huang Pu River a formalized frontal posture honoring the architectural traditions of the adjacent historic Central Bund.

A podium moving from five to eight levels provides the 102,000-square-meter office and retail complex with its unifying element, and anchors it at street level to the neighborhood, while the towers rise to pedestrian bridges linking public open spaces and crossing Zhongshan Road to Huang Pu River.

1

1   Model view from the north
2   Site plan
3   West tower, high-rise plan
4   West tower, mid-rise plan
5   East tower, high-rise plan
6   East tower, mid-rise plan
7   Model view from the south

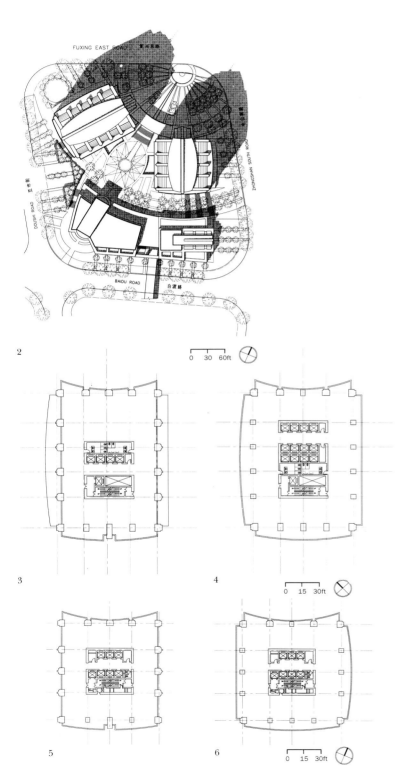

2

0 30 60ft

3

4

0 15 30ft

5

6

0 15 30ft

7

The McConnell Foundation

Design/Completion 1993/1997
Redding, California
The McConnell Foundation
36,000 square feet (150-acre site)
Exposed Douglas fir timbers; stone floors; copper roof

Located on a 150-acre site with five lakes, this small headquarters building is built on a dam between two of the lakes and commands views of the nearby mountains of northern California.

The building is approached across a gracious cobbled granite entry plaza surrounded by open sun-shading arcades and a meeting pavilion. The structure is of recycled old-growth Douglas fir with stone floors and a copper roof.

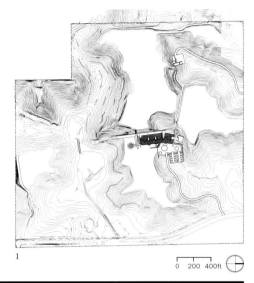

1

0   200   400ft

2

1   Site plan
2   East façade model (partial)
3   Model, roof study (partial)
4   Entry plaza at east façade

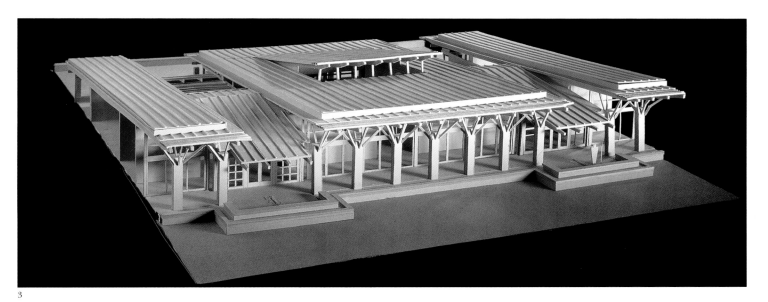

3

4

Tulalip Cultural Museum

Design/Completion 1995/1997
Marysville, Washington
The Tulalip Tribes
43,900 square feet
Concrete columns; glue-laminated beams; cedar walls

The Tulalip Indian tribe asked the design team to "capture the essence of the longhouse," their traditional gathering place. Large structural members, cedar walls, vast space, and light filtering through apertures at the ridge of a simple roof are to them the most significant characteristics.

Built of concrete columns and glue-laminated beams, the museum adopts the construction logic of the original longhouse. The seasonal nature of the tribe is reflected in the expression of the structure in the landscape. The exposed structure of walls and roof recall the longhouse during summer when, stripped of its cedar planks, the log frames stood exposed.

The museum is divided into three programmatic zones: artifact processing and administration (archives); galleries (past/present); library and classrooms (learning/future). These zones are bridged by skylit exhibit corridors of great height for the display of artifacts.

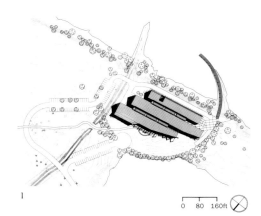

1

0   80   160ft

2

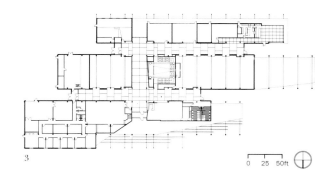

3

0   25   50ft

4

5

Hyatt Regency Hotel Addition

Design/Completion 1995/on hold
Columbus, Ohio
Ohio Center Hotel Co., Ltd
192,000 gross square feet
Steel structure; precast concrete
Aluminum curtain wall

Anchoring the northern end of the downtown business district in Columbus, this 300-room addition to the existing Hyatt Regency Hotel occupies a small, restricted triangular site at the entry to the existing hotel. Maintaining views from existing hotel rooms and retaining the existing entry and lobby were important considerations.

The new Hyatt Regency addition is located at the corner of a major urban intersection which it addresses at a 45-degree angle, consistent with structures on the other corners. Its narrow configuration preserves views from the existing hotel and offers new vistas of the historical area to the north and the central city to the south.

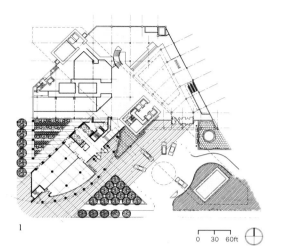

1

0   30   60ft

2

1   Site plan
2   View from the southwest
3   Typical floor plan
4   Southeast elevation
5   Southwest elevation
6   Northwest elevation

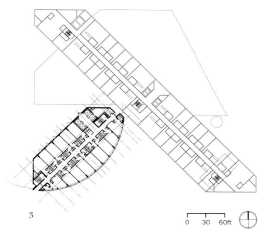

3

0   30   60ft

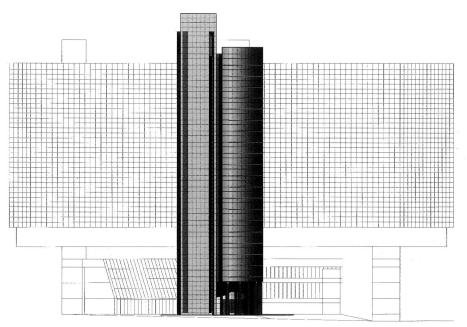

5

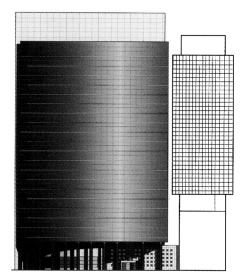

4

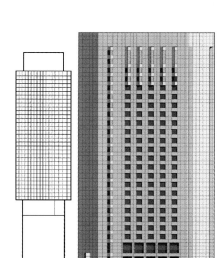

6

Dayton Cultural and Commercial Center

Design 1996
Dayton, Ohio
Second & Main Ltd/ Downtown Dayton Partnership
850,000 square feet
Winning competition entry

Located on an important site in the center of Dayton, this mixed-use project is the key to an emerging renaissance in this aerospace city famed as the home of the Wright Brothers.

While the office building tower, housing, and parking conform to the rigid orthogonal grid of the surrounding area, the 2,200-seat performing arts theater and 100-room luxury hotel take on fluid and dynamic forms, subtly recalling Dayton's aerospace heritage while enlivening the city center. The space between hotel, theater, and office is enclosed as an atrium that serves all three.

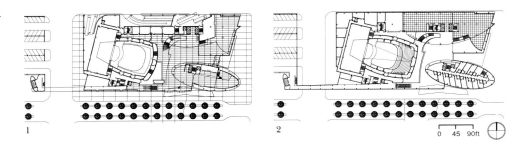

1   2   0   45   90ft

3

1   Ground level plan
2   Level two, mezzanine plan
3   Aerial view of model from the southeast
4   Street level view from the southeast

78

4

EBH Bodi Tower

Design/Completion 1995/1999
Ulaanbaatar, Mongolia
EBH Bodi Financial Services (Mongolia) Ltd
25 stories: 40,508 square meters (436,033 square feet)
Concrete structure
Glass/metal panel exterior

This 25-story office building in Ulaanbaatar is the first skyline symbol of Mongolia's leap into the global marketplace. The tower incorporates state-of-the-art technology to accommodate the developer's specific request that its offices meet or exceed the expectations of the international companies that will tenant the building.

Adopting the rounded contours of the *ger*, the traditional dwelling of Mongolia's desert culture, the tower offers a curved face to the robust winds of the northwest region. The *ger* is more literally alluded to at the street-level Opar Plaza, with its round two-story rotunda sheathed in glass at the southwest corner. The Mongolian past finds further reference in a sculpture of eight running horses, beasts which were a vital part of traditional nomadic culture.

The uppermost floors feature a members' club offering the latest appointments for relaxation and entertainment. A top floor observation platform affords residents and visitors an unprecedented vista of the city and surrounding countryside.

1   Typical office floor plan
2   View from the south

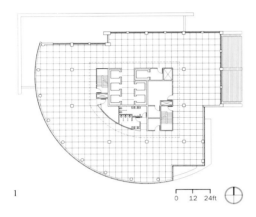

1

2

Jakarta Mixed-Use Tower

Design 1996
Jakarta, Indonesia
Pt. Binapuri Lestari
60 stories of office, 500-room four-star hotel, 1,000-car parking,
renovation of existing 12-story building
Composite steel/concrete structure
Glass curtain wall
Winning competition entry

This 80-story mixed-use complex is located in Jakarta's prominent Golden Triangle district. The shimmering tower leans out from its base and then curves skyward, giving the building a sensual and unusual perspective both from street level and from a distance.

The lower part of the tower is dedicated to hotel use, with the adjacent retail space in an existing building enveloped by a giant video screen. Films, video clips, and advertisements projected on the screen generate interest and excitement at the entrance level. Above this is an unusual fin-shaped room with towering glass walls which can be used as a ballroom or conference center.

The upper part of the tower houses office space from which double-decker elevators provide access to a series of sky atriums with spectacular views.

1

2

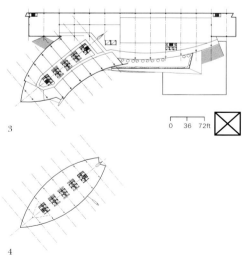

3

4

1   Aerial view
2   Office floors at top of tower
3   Hotel lobby level
4   Typical office floor plan

CORPORATE INTERIORS

GNA Corporate Headquarters

Design/Completion 1989
Seattle, Washington
Great Northern Insured Annuity
134,000 square feet (8 floors)

Complex philosophical challenges inspired elegant design solutions for the corporate headquarters of Great Northern Insured Annuity. A progressive company enjoying rapid expansion, GNA wanted a humane, engaging employee environment with functional flexibility to accommodate future growth at minimum cost. NBBJ responded with an open-office plan that playfully stretches traditional modular workstation dynamics.

Ethospace systems form a fanning pattern with their spines perpendicular to the central core on each of eight floors, thus preserving the unique curves of the Two Union Square tower and its splendid views of downtown Seattle, Elliott Bay, and the mountain ranges surrounding the city. Circulation perimeters establish vantage points for these vistas as well as easy office access and conversation areas. Adjustable, interchangeable components allow employees to relocate between workstation neighborhoods and personalize their spaces with ease.

1   Executive suite floor plan
2   Typical workstation floor plan
3   Conference area with view
4   Executive suite reception area

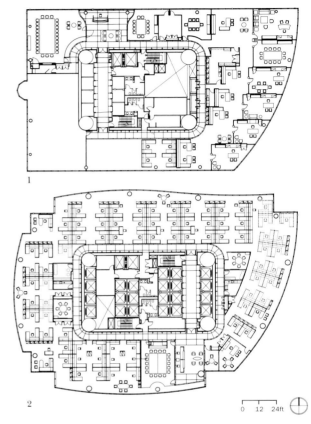

1

2

0   12   24ft

3

84

4

Seafirst Gallery

Design/Completion 1993
Seattle, Washington
Seafirst Bank
2,700 square feet

Creating a highly flexible gallery for the display of art in an irregular space located in a high-rise office tower was the design challenge of Seafirst Gallery. Display panels pivot around steel support columns placed off-center within each panel, allowing 8-inch-diameter bronze spheres at the panel ends to inscribe arcs of different radii on the hardwood floor. Shallow bronze tracks record the arcs with sinuous patterns on the floor. Ironwood handles at the ends of each partition withdraw cane bolts from strikes in the floor when lowered, and serve as levers for rotating the panels.

1

1 Pivoting display walls
2 Cast bronze spherical caster design schematic
3 Cane bolt and cast bronze caster detail
4 Schematics of primary partition configurations
5 Alternating fan wall configuration

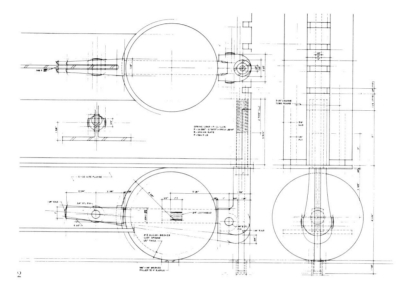

2

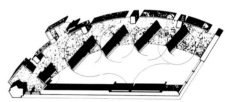

3

4

Herring Newman Offices

Design/Completion 1990/1991
Seattle, Washington
Herring Newman Direct Response Marketing Company
17,000 square feet
Stock construction materials: pre-fabricated wood trusses;
corrugated fiberglass; plywood; framing lumber; chainlink fencing;
perforated metal mesh; raw steel; copper and concrete;
whitewashed chipboard; builder's felt; galvanized pan decking

This national direct mail advertising agency sought an office design that would inspire employees, clients, and vendors to "feel that anything is possible—a place in which solutions have no boundaries and conventional wisdom has no place." Specifically, Herring Newman wanted an atmosphere that gave its workers "permission to think 'outside the box' and encourage creativity in every aspect of their jobs."

That remarkable challenge was met first with site selection: the third and fourth floors of a historic, five-story flatiron in downtown Seattle that had once housed the city's daily newspaper. Taking its cue from the building's triangular shape, the two-story office complex avoids inter-floor separation with a large, open triangle that joins the floors visually and acoustically. A spiral stair of raw milled steel ascends on axis with the center of the opening, which serves as both the nucleus for art layout and center stage for the firm's creative process.

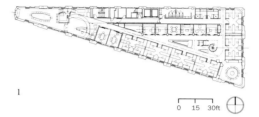

1

0 15 30ft

2

3

1 Floor plan, lobby level
2 Reception lobby
3 Central production area

Burger King Corporate World Headquarters

Design/Completion 1992/1993
Miami, Florida
Burger King Corporation
300,000 square feet on four floors
Translucent glass curtain walls

After Hurricane Andrew devastated downtown Miami in the fall of 1992, leaving only the roof and structural frame of Burger King's headquarters, the fast food giant took the opportunity to review its corporate culture and operations, and renew both with renovated headquarters offices.

Burger King's new plan contributes to a strong corporate community environment. An adjacency strategy redistributes executive offices from an isolated cluster to proximity with their specific employee group or division, each in turn positioned near other related or interdependent groups or divisions.

Imaginative integration of color and pattern reinforce the urban plan concept by delineating "Main Streets" and "Neighborhoods" with distinctive mixes of shapes and hues drawn from the elements of Burger King's product: mustard, ketchup, lettuce, tomatoes, pickles.

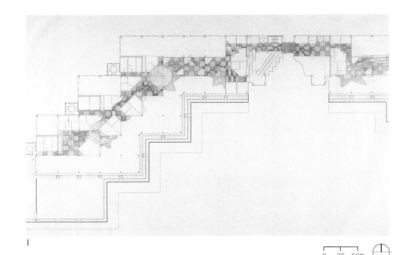

1

0 25 50ft

2

1   Typical floor plan with carpet plan
2   "Main Street"
3   Conference room off "Main Street"

Herman Miller Regional Sales Office and Showroom

Design 1995
Seattle, Washington
Herman Miller
4,500 square feet
Cork flooring; non-endangered wood veneers; non-toxic finishes;
laminate-faced sliding doors

The program for this furnishings company was both direct and oblique: provide office space suitable for eight regional representatives, yet in an atmosphere conducive to showcasing the diverse Herman Miller merchandise. The classic Meisian office tower chosen by the company as its new home offered an appropriate setting for displaying its product line of custom systems furniture and accessories: an attractive and efficient office presenting and representing important and effective office products.

The design solution illustrates the dual nature of the facility as office and showroom by integrating existing architectural features with new construction, and realizing furnishings as architectural elements inspired by Herman Miller's own designs.

1

2

3

1 Reception/gallery
2 Product display corridor
3 Conference room door detail
4 Entry/product display

4

Starbucks Coffee Company Urban Campus

Design/Completion 1993/present
Seattle, Washington
Starbucks Coffee Company
360,000 square feet
Brick, concrete, natural wood

When Starbucks Coffee Company decided to move its corporate home to a stout old warehouse building in Seattle's industrial area, it provided the opportunity to give the building and its 17-acre site a new life, and to encourage the development of new office, retail, and residential development in the area.

The project organized the façades of the existing buildings, added an elevator core and mechanical/electrical infrastructure, developed green spaces, and built out three floors of office space.

Worn brick, concrete, natural wood and tropical colors borrowed from Starbucks retail graphics animate the office space. The 120,000-square-foot floor plates are organized around diagonal corridors fronted by conference, copy, and informal lounge rooms, and coffee rooms serving Starbucks' own rich brews. The corridors intersect at a central commons on each floor where the company's young employees gather to share the excitement of its latest incursion into the international retail marketplace.

1

1   Stair detail
2   Roasting and tasting area
3   Lounge
4   Typical connecting stair

2

3

4

HEALTH CARE

Scottsdale Memorial Hospital North Pavilion

Design/Completion 1981/1983 (Phase I), 1983/1989 (Phase II)
Scottsdale, Arizona
Scottsdale Memorial Hospital
Phase I: 3 stories, 164,340 gross square feet, 120 beds
Phase II: 5 stories, 225,000 gross square feet
Cast-in-place concrete walls with stucco or gypsum surfaces, metal deck

With the growth of Scottsdale's central hospital constrained by its site, a new facility was required to serve the burgeoning leisure community some 9 miles northeast of downtown. Sited on 38.5 acres bisected by an arroyo (dry stream bed), the new hospital called for a flexible design that could be constructed in stages over several years, yet would stand apparently complete at each stage.

Noted by *Progressive Architecture* for its "skillful contextualism," SMH North presents a relaxed, almost resort-style façade derived from the patterns and hues of the indigenous desert culture. The east façade is protected from intense morning sun by deep recesses that screen the windows and create a rich play of light and shadow. The western areas of the building remain windowless against the searing afternoon sun.

On the inside it is a modern health care facility, the transition from desert sun to welcoming reception area accented by a
Continued

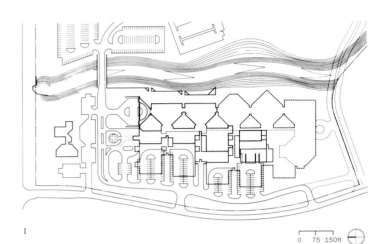

1

0   75   150ft

2

1   Site plan
2   Typical courtyard
3   View from the northeast
4   Entry level floor plan

98

3

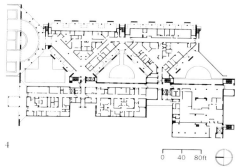

4

portico that veils the main entrance in
cool shadows. A central circulation spine
organizes the triangular complex; nursing
units cluster along this north–south
avenue and establish entries to various
departments, which can respond
independently to workload changes
for immediate and long-range expansion.

Phase I established a primary health care
hospital with 120 beds, four operatories
and X-ray rooms, an emergency
department, and food services with
cafeteria.

The private patient rooms promote
the facility's reassuring atmosphere,
with special attention paid to comfort,
ambience, view, and light to minimize
the institutional qualities typical of most
hospitals. Vistas of surrounding deserts

Continued

5

6

5 East façade
6 Detail showing façade layering
7 East façade at stair

7

and distant mountains are emphasized wherever possible, and triangular internal courtyards permit sunlight and comforting views.

Appended directly to the south of the initial buildings, Phase II more than doubled the facility to 262 beds and 14 operatories. At fulfillment of the master plan, SMH North will again double to comprise 500 beds in a comprehensive care facility.

8

9

8   Distant view of west façade
9   Window detail
10   Entry court

102

10

Central Washington Hospital
Additions and Alterations

Design/Completion 1990/1992
Wenatchee, Washington
Central Washington Hospital
200,000 square feet
(38,971 square feet new; 27,000 square feet remodel)
65,971 square feet new work in 200,000 square feet total site
Integrally colored stucco over load-bearing concrete block
(treatment areas), clear glass with clear anodized
aluminum mullions (lobbies)

This regional hospital serving a four-county area in eastern Washington's orchard belt has more than doubled in size during each of its three decades of operation. NBBJ was commissioned to address further growth with two major additions and a main facility renovation.

The one-story 9,500-square-foot Ambulatory Surgery Wing (ASW) accommodates same-day interventive care (a growing trend in hospital services in which patients are admitted, undergo treatment, recuperate, and return home in a single day). Sited with its companion Emergency Treatment Facility (ETF) in the existing hospital's northwest corner, the ASW comprises a central nursing area organized around a rotunda, and 22 single-bed recovery rooms that face onto two interior courtyards.

Continued

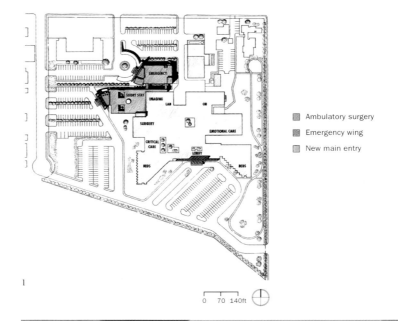

1

Ambulatory surgery
Emergency wing
New main entry

0   70   140ft

1   Site plan with hospital growth diagrams
2   Main entrance detail showing canopy and anodized aluminum letters
3   Ambulatory surgery wing entry arcade
4   Ground floor plan for new additions
5   Surgery entrance with Emergency Treatment Facility in left background

2

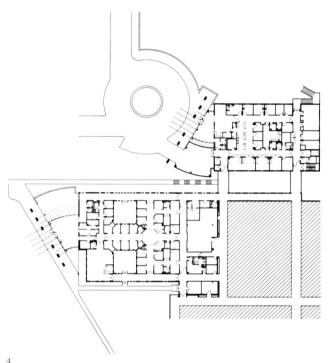

3

4

5

These private rooms, smaller and homier than typical recovery wards, assure comfort and ready access to supervising nurses, while taking full advantage of the pleasant mountain views and the recuperative effects of flora and sunlight.

High-ceiling wedge-shaped waiting areas in both the ASW and ETF derive from space left between the new octagonal wings and their angled entry walls. With three sides of floor-to-ceiling glass windows, the lobbies are sunny public spaces that provide views through the identifying entry wall to landscaped areas and nearby landmarks.

The two-story 7,500-square-foot Emergency Treatment Facility, which extends north from the hospital proper, triples CWH's emergency department, providing 12 treatment stations, four large trauma rooms, two small emergency treatment rooms, and substantial office space on the main floor. The upper floor emergency services divide into walk-in patient care on the wing's north side, ambulance patient care on the south side,

Continued

6

6   Surgery rotunda at control desk
7   Emergency entrance with ambulatory surgery
     beyond
8   Ambulatory surgery with garden court
9   South elevation, ambulatory surgery

7

8

9

and nursing stations and support areas at the center for efficient staffing and maximum supervisory control. At the main floor level, office, reception, and waiting areas all have courtyard views.

The most dramatic changes on the site are the three 34-foot stucco entry walls that designate the two-wing additions and the main facility; these elements lend both unity and a sophisticated new image through a distinctive architectural symbol.

Deriving their colors from the orchard fruit of the Wenatchee region, these vibrant walls clearly identify the hospital's three primary entrances and lend a distinctive character to the overall complex.

10

10   Night view of entries with mountain backdrop
11   Detail, ambulatory surgery

11

Pomona Valley Hospital and Medical Center Women's Center

Design/Completion 1988/1992
Pomona, California
Pomona Valley Hospital and Medical Center
190,000 gross square feet (133,000 net square feet)
Sandstone, precast concrete panels

As the first of five phases in Pomona Valley Hospital's replacement and expansion master plan, the Women's Center establishes the facility's architectural framework and provides integrated inpatient and outpatient services for women and newborns. The center weds alternative birthing concepts and modern technology for a home-birth ambience with optimal medical support. Challenged to provide a gracious, comfortable environment accessible to a diverse clientele, the plan adopts a non-institutional appearance and straightforward circulation pattern.

A red sandstone base underlies the building's cream-colored precast concrete panels. Windows include large precast surrounds with cool green patina finishes and white accents. Main public circulation routes follow perimeter walls, enhancing orientation and providing abundant natural light.

The 190,000-square-foot facility takes special account of the sunny climate with interior courtyards that provide cool,
Continued

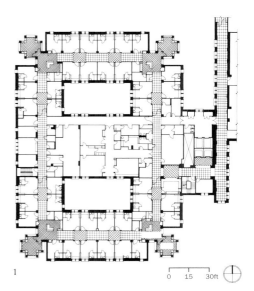

1   Typical birthing floor plan
2   Main entrance
3   Connecting gallery to hospital with corner "porch" beyond
4   Exterior balcony at interior courtyard

3

4

tranquil spaces for relaxation and natural light for interior patient rooms. Each of the 26 birthing suites contains a small inglenook for family members and a bed, fully but unobtrusively equipped for birthing, that can be curtained off for privacy or in emergencies. Head walls of sliding fabric and cherry trim panels allow immediate access to otherwise hidden gas, power, and telemetry connections.

The inglenook has a large, broad window with inset sofa bed and retractable table that folds into surrounding woodwork. The niche allows family members to gather without disturbing the mother, and provides a comfortable setting for celebratory dinners.

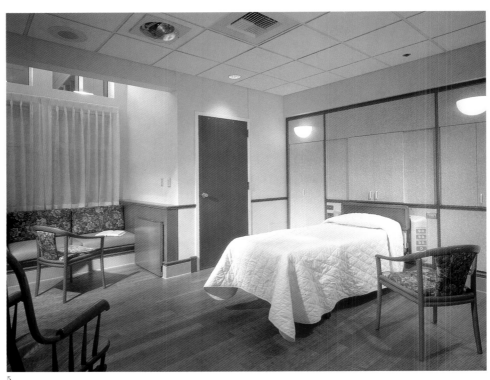
5

6

7

5 Typical labor/delivery/recovery/post-partum
   room
6 Interior courtyard
7 Sitting area
8 Night view of the connecting gallery from a corner
   "porch"

Children's Hospital and Health Center Patient Care Pavilion

Design/Completion 1989/1993
San Diego, California
Children's Hospital and Health Center
187,000 square feet
Stucco, terra cotta

This new 187,000-square-foot addition to San Diego's prestigious Children's Hospital answers simultaneously several key issues. In addition to alleviating severe crowding at the 40-year-old hospital, addressing the specific needs of pediatric care, and announcing a fresh image to its community, the 114-bed Patient Care Pavilion embodies a unique vision for health care in creating an environment specially tuned to the sensibilities of its patients.

The pavilion incorporates playful forms and details that mollify the traditional institutional character of hospitals that can so frighten children. The 29.5-acre campus comprises inviting human-scale elements in the familiar shapes of the architectural forms of the surrounding culture: ample windows in lively articulated façades of sandy stucco (with darker, patterned masonry at the base); pitched metal roofs in warm terra cotta tones (reminiscent of the landmark Hotel del Coronado); chimney-shaped ventilation cores; a playful 60-foot clock

Continued

1

0 20 40ft

2

1 Site plan
2 East entry façade (from across a freeway)
3 Exterior stair and courtyard balcony

3

tower; patios; and eight landscaped courtyards. Designed to comfort children arriving at the hospital, such engaging details continue throughout the facility: the first floor lobby's circular reception desk (finished in stainless steel and plastic laminate) appears much like a toy drum.

"The philosophy that happy kids heal better and faster is what this place is all about," CHHC President Blair Sadler has said of the pavilion. "It's a place that expresses healing, where families know they're getting the best care possible."

The first floor includes outpatient clinics, a gift shop, and the vibrant parti-colored Children's Way Cafe (announced in glowing neon). The second floor is organized around 30-bed nursing sections presented as distinct neighborhoods of 10-bed clusters of "houses." Nursing stations at the center of each neighborhood allow immediate access to each child, accentuate the pavilion's human scale, and emphasize a residential atmosphere that encourages the relaxation and sociability essential to

Continued

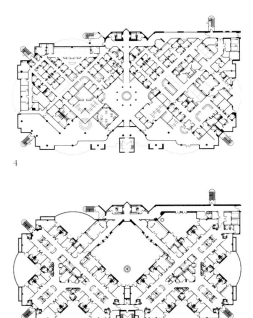

4

5

0   25   50ft

6

7

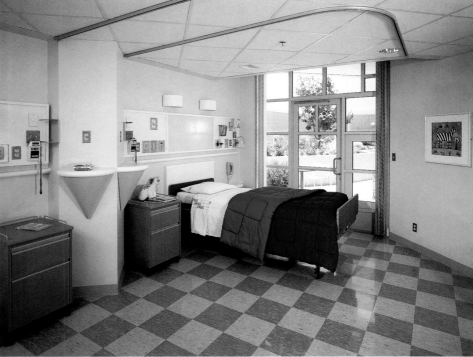

8

recovery. Each distinct station comprises a "garden courtyard" of reception and administrative space fronting an office "house" with peaked roof and chimney-shaped mechanical spaces. Globe lights provide cool moonlighting accented with twinkling fiber-optic "constellations" (unique to each floor) in the ceiling. This neighborhood format helps to diminish the building mass, and insures natural lighting throughout the facility. Second-floor playcourts open to the sunlight give children a place to recuperate with outdoor play. Each room retains state-of-the-art medical technology, albeit artfully concealed: head wall spaces for oxygen and other necessities are shaped like ice-cream cones.

Individual rooms carry the atmosphere of home further with bright colors (each door different for easy identification), personal cabinets and work counters in geometric forms reinforcing the overall design, marker boards and a selection of decorative artwork to help personalize each room, and televisions and VCRs recessed in columns echoing the pavilion's landmark clock tower.

9

10

9   Children's Way Cafe
10   Family waiting room
11   Elevation, central courtyard

11

12

12 Downspout details
13 Typical nursing station with fibre-optic star field
   overhead

13

Aultman Hospital Addition and Renovation

Design/Completion 1991/1994
Canton, Ohio
Aultman Hospital
125,932 square feet
Brick, steel
Glass curtain wall

Seeking both harmony and revitalization with the addition of a new wing and parking garage, the design team used an altered geometry, extensive glass, and large new lanterns while carefully incorporating details, color, and materials used in the existing buildings.

Site design and landscape are carefully coordinated to enhance way-finding on the campus, and to provide secluded seating in small courts and gardens. This is particularly noticeable along the south façade where site design elements also serve to conceal underground mechanical equipment.

1

2

1   Site plan
2   View looking northeast to new surgery addition
3   Small sculpture court adjacent to main entry court
4   Exterior courtyards and walkway along south façade

4

3

Harrison Memorial Hospital Patient Registration and Surgery Expansion

Design/Completion 1993/1995
Bremerton, Washington
Harrison Memorial Hospital
3 stories: 54,000 square feet
Concrete and splitface limestone

The only site available for expansion of the increasingly crowded Harrison Memorial Hospital was a courtyard formed by its three existing wings, each representing distinct architectural styles and diluting any sense of unity. Early conversations with hospital administrators revealed a clear interest in enlivening and unifying the facility's identity as well as expanding its capability. The subsequent three-story addition to the Patient Registration and Surgery included improvements to the facility's basement, ground, and first floors that significantly increased its operational capacity and unified its appearance and circulation routes.

Functionally, the project comprises a new patient registration lobby and waiting area and seven new operating rooms. Service areas for the new operating rooms include patient interview rooms and waiting areas, outpatient pre-operatory exam rooms, office space for surgery personnel, and warehouse loading and storage space.

Continued

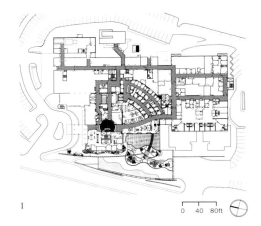

1

0   40   80ft

2

1   Site plan
2   Covered terrace
3   Ground floor plan
4   Surgery floor plan
5   West elevation

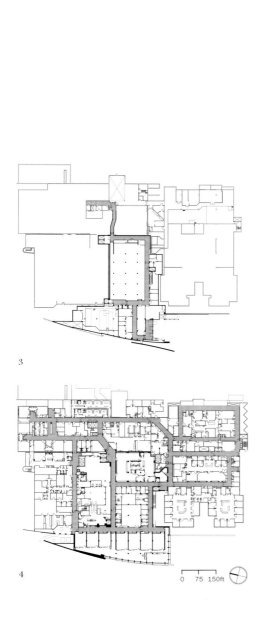

3

4

0 75 150ft

5

The interior atmosphere reflects the staff's commitment to welcoming the community in a comfortable patient-focused setting. A light-filled waiting area with a focal fireplace creates a non-institutional atmosphere unlike any hospital reception area in the region. A large landscaped roof terrace abuts the lobby, offering a protected outdoor waiting area with views of mountains and water, reinforcing the hospital's patient-focused philosophy by integrating daylight, landscape, and access to fresh air.

This new addition provides a strong visual base that unifies the campus with a consistent structural gesture, a series of curving landscaped walls. The effect of supporting the existing wings with a series of related landscape elements achieved the required spatial expansion yet mitigated the massing of a new addition.

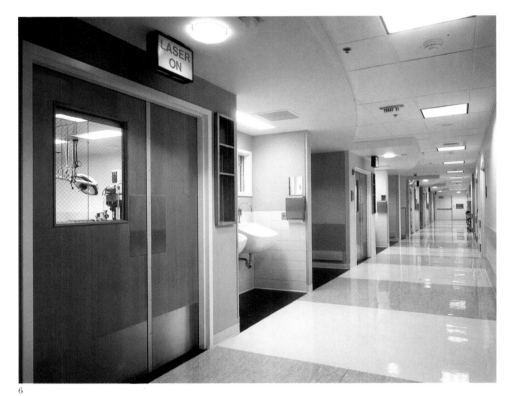

6

7

8

6   Surgery corridor
7&8   Terrace detail

Providence Medical Center East Wing Expansion

Design/Completion 1988/1991
Seattle, Washington
Providence Medical Center (Sisters of Providence)
7 stories: 138,000 gross square feet/120,000 net square feet
Brick with steel framing

This seven-story tower successfully responded to a number of difficult design challenges: containing a large program (five units of 36 single beds) within a small site; complementing a nearby landmark beloved to hospital staff and the local community; replacing the original Providence Hall, built in 1929; meeting stringent setback requirements; joining new patient, staff, and supply circulation to an existing patchwork of elevators and pathways; and improving PMC's image and position within the competitive health care market. A compact plan solved all these concerns while providing superior services in acute medical, surgical, and psychiatric care. Special concern for pedestrian distances and window and street setbacks were simultaneously addressed.

The PMC East Wing takes visual cues from the adjacent 1910 building. The highly modeled wing recalls the tripartite massing, materials, colors, and fenestration, not by reproducing them but by recasting them as crisp textural juxtapositions that also suggest the state-of-the-art technology within.

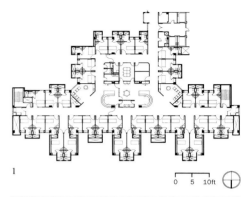

1

2

3

1   Typical nursing floor plan
2   North elevation
3   View of northeast corner

Moore Regional Hospital Health and Wellness Center

Design/Completion 1992/1995
Pinehurst, North Carolina
Moore Regional Hospital
48,571 square feet
Brick, painted steel, precast concrete columns
Glass curtain wall

Situated on a knoll overlooking Moore Regional Hospital, the MRH Health and Wellness Center combines recreational and clinical facilities particularly geared to sports and fitness in a building with colors, materials, and massing that reflect its southern heritage.

Recreation facilities comprise the majority of the center's 48,571 square feet, with weight training, an aerobics studio, a combined volleyball and basketball court, an indoor running track, three racquetball courts, a 25-yard pool for competition and leisure, a whirlpool, and a sauna room. Clinical services affiliated with the hospital consist of patient evaluation and treatment rooms for physical, occupational, and cardiac rehabilitation therapy. Public spaces include a lobby and lounge with a juice bar, lockers, a pro shop, and a child care room.

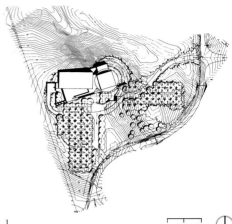

1

2

1　Site plan
2　View from the east
3　First floor plan
4　Second floor plan
5　View from the southeast

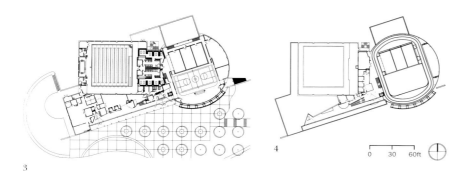

3

4

0 30 60ft

5

Alaska Native Medical Center

Design/Completion 1991/1996
Anchorage, Alaska
United States Public Health Service
380,635 square feet over several structures
Steel structure, brick exterior, precast membrane, copper, and turn-coated steel roofs, storefront glazing and punched windows, skywall for entry canopy and steel structure

The largest project ever undertaken by the US Public Health Services, this 380,635-square-foot replacement facility serves as a regional medical center for the native peoples of Alaska. Comprising 150 acute care beds, a 59-bed hostel, and the Center for Disease Control Arctic Investigations Lab, ANMC fulfills a severe need for advanced medical care while remaining sensitive to the modest scale, intimate nature, and distinct values of the local culture. Aware that many native residents had never seen large structures, and sensitive to capturing the deep sense of community, NBBJ designers researched Native Alaskan life and art for 18 months before beginning their conceptual design.

Villagers and tribes were assured participation in all formal reviews and presentations throughout the design process through the Community Central Design Committee. From initial to final concept, native communities were asked to recommend ways to tailor the end product to the specialized needs of their people.
Continued

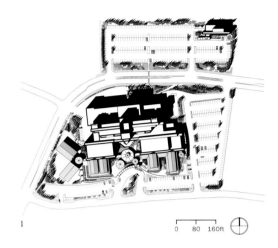

1

0   80   160ft

2

1 Site plan
2 Exterior Detail
3 View from the west
4 Cross section looking east

3

4

0 15 30ft

ANMC responds to cultural cues by creating a series of warm, friendly gathering spaces throughout the facility. Areas focused around a central point are characteristic of native cultures. Thus, the hospital's main lobby adopts the form and atmosphere of a community hall or lodge where people can meet and socialize with family and friends. Upper level lobbies emphasize gathering space and the region's spectacular mountain views—visually delightful to all patients but especially important to Native Alaskans, who frequently orient themselves using natural landmarks.

The complex steps back to the north to allow daylight to flood its interiors, and to de-emphasize its scale and reduce its apparent mass. A series of one-story pavilions with sloped roofs cluster along the front of the center to establish a village-like setting more familiar in scale and appearance to most Native Alaskans. This important design decision, a direct reference to the traditional Tlingit Whale House, makes the building less intimidating.

Continued

5

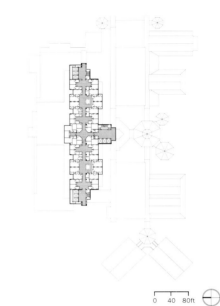

6

0   40   80ft

7

8

9

Direct imitation of the traditional forms and styles of Native Alaskan architecture, arts, and crafts was avoided, the architects choosing rather to evoke the familiar by understanding its underlying principles. For instance, entrances with expressed structural frame canopies recall the whalebone-frame structures of Inupiak communities. The colored brickwork patterning of ANMC's exterior stitches together the facility's mass and form in an abstract reference to the Athabascan tradition of emphasizing seams and joints with intricate ornamental designs. (In their clothing, watertight seams are essential to survival.) Elsewhere the brickwork and sloping roofs suggest the gabled sod-brick *barabaras* of the Aleuts.

10

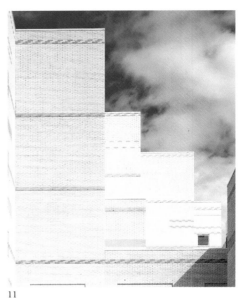

11

12

10 Meditation space
11 Detail of brick pattern
12 View from the east
13 View from the northwest
14 Detail at employee entrance

13

14

Swedish Medical Center Southeast Wing Addition

Design/Completion 1992/1996
Seattle, Washington
Swedish Medical Center
671,000 square feet
Precast concrete panels with granite aggregate and silver-finished metal

The Southeast Wing takes its gestural curves from its site, a nexus between Seattle's downtown and First Hill districts. A convex crescent, the tower's primary façade, presents a sturdy presence on the skyline of this hilly city. The embracing concave curve of the three-story base welcomes patients, families, and staff. The center of the complex is established by the entry rotunda dome, 24 feet in diameter, which is internally lit for a memorable welcome.

The building program comprises the entrance and lobby rotunda; ambulatory care; a pharmacy; an intensive care unit; 24 operating rooms with recovery, interventional and imaging areas; special care nurseries; labor delivery recovery suites; 180 nursing beds; central supply; and underground parking for 600 automobiles.

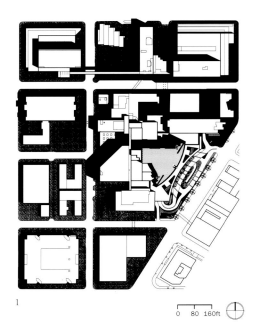

1

0   80 160ft

2

3

136

1 Site plan
2 Rendering showing completed tower
3 Phase I, main entrance
4 Detail
5 First floor plan
6 View at main lobby
7 Entrance rotunda

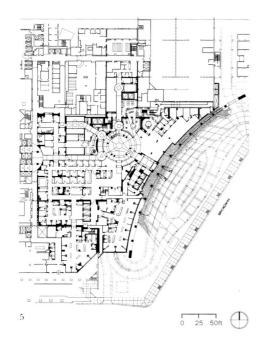

Masan Samsung Hospital

Design/Completion 1995/2000
Masan, South Korea
Samsung Corporation
74,530 square meters (800,000 square feet)
Concrete and steel composite structural system
Winning competition entry

This 800,000-square-foot facility will provide diagnostic services and referral support for other hospitals in Masan Province, as well as 700 acute and intensive care beds and a regional center for nursing education.

The campus design expresses the owner's corporate philosophy of clarity, simplicity, and order, in the relationship of functional parts to unified whole and the relationship of architectural mass to landscape. The striking double-curved tower takes its airfoil-like shape from its site: it stands in a narrow valley with hills channeling wind around it on either side. The tower will serve as a regional beacon for patients who, once inside, will encounter clear pathways to services in a simply ordered healing environment.

1

2

3

1 Courtyard view from the southeast
2 Outpatient clinic lobby
3 Outpatient clinic level
4 Transverse section
5 Typical inpatient floor
6 Outpatient clinics
7 Perspective view from the north

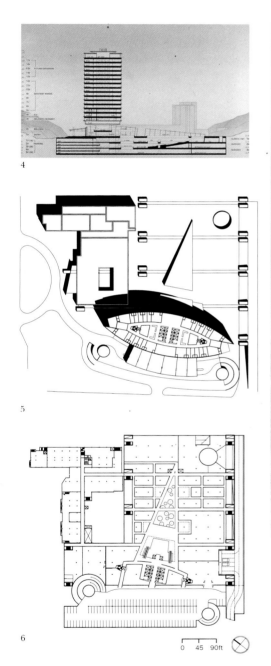

4

5

6

0 45 90ft

7

Kangbuk Samsung Hospital

Design/Completion 1995/1999
Seoul, South Korea
Samsung Corporation
900,000 square feet (83,643 square meters)
Stainless steel panels, stone, glass, metal
Winning competition entry

Kangbuk Samsung Hospital overcomes complexity to create a clear statement about place, order, and access to modern health care. It makes a single, clear visual statement of its purpose and importance in a dense urban neighborhood, and it combines three elegant building forms with the existing Boyoung Tower. It further accommodates a complex functional program while offering patients and visitors graceful access and clear paths to their destinations.

The external form of the hospital expresses the integration of its functional parts, and the means of access to each. The four bundled towers are clearly joined, yet at the point of connection invite daylight to pass between.

1

1   Aerial view looking west (model)
2   Section looking west
3   Site plan
4   Typical tower plan
5   Aerial perspective
6   Atrium interior
7   Interior view at entry

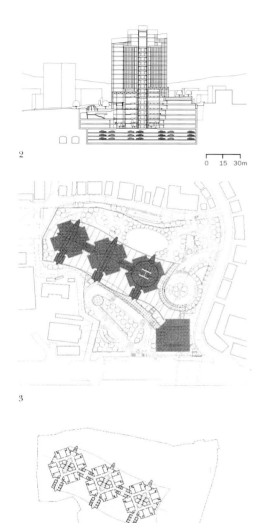

2

0 15 30m

3

4

0 15 30m

5

6

7

Rainbow Babies' and Children's Hospital Renovations and Bed Tower Additions

Design/Completion 1995/1998
Cleveland, Ohio
University Hospitals of Cleveland
189,000 square feet new; 44,000 square feet renovation
Brick, metal, and glass

A world-renowned pediatric hospital pioneering family-centered health care, Rainbow Babies' and Children's Hospital addressed its severe need for renewal with major renovations including a state-of-the-art 175-bed tower addition.

With the aim of providing a positive healing environment supportive of children's physical, social, and developmental needs, the RBCH renovation was planned to appeal to children while acknowledging family needs and accommodating changes in health care delivery.

Each floor is organized into small communities (distributed according to age or acuity) with entertaining themes drawn from the community to nurture a sense of familiarity and belonging for patients and families. Playrooms on each floor overlook an interior courtyard that invites natural light into the hospital.

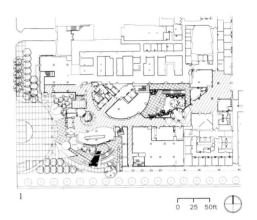

1

0 25 50ft

2

3

0 25 50ft

1   Site plan
2   View from the east
3   Typical floor plan

Genesys Regional Medical Center

Design/Completion 1992/1997
Grand Blanc, Michigan
Genesys Health System
820,000 square feet on a 440-acre site
Steel frame
Burnish block and EIFS exterior
Winning competition entry

GRMC merges four traditional hospitals into a unified complex. This $90 million health care park comprises seven individual diagnostic and treatment centers grouped around a four-story landscaped atrium with all destination points in full view.

Designed as a fully integrated medical campus, GRMC aligns 100,000 square feet of physician offices with their respective diagnostic and treatment areas. For instance, open-heart surgeons can enter the cardiac catheterization lab directly from their individual office suites.

Each center acts as an independent mini-hospital totally responsible for all the care needs of its patients, and fully equipped with inpatient/outpatient facilities, procedure space, diagnostic imaging, laboratory, and pharmacy.

1

0   40   80ft

2

1   Typical floor plan
2   Aerial view from the southwest

Koo Foundation Cancer Center

Design/Completion 1993/1997
Kwan Tu (near Taipei), Taiwan, Republic of China
Koo Foundation
700,000 square feet (577,000 square feet of medical facility, the
rest parking): 7 floors above ground and 2 below
Concrete frame
Curtain wall, ceramic tile exterior

Taiwan's first comprehensive cancer care
facility blends innovative Western health
care systems with culturally sensitive
patterns of use in a healing environment
organized around principles of feng shui,
the Chinese philosophy of spatial
harmony.

Recognizing natural light and landscape
as essential to the healing process, the
design solution for the 577,000-square foot
facility achieves a complementary
relationship between natural setting and
created element for an atmosphere of
peace and well-being. Located northeast
of Taipei at Kwan Tu at the edge of Yan
Ming Shan National Park, the Center
opens to the lush tropical landscape of
the foothills surrounding the Tamshui
River basin.

The central lobby/atrium focuses on
an exterior garden with a waterfall that
encourages quiet reflection.

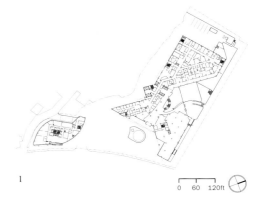

1

0   60   120ft

2

1   Site plan
2   View from the south

University of Rochester, Ambulatory Care Center

Design/Completion 1992/1996
Rochester, New York
University of Rochester
321,000 square feet
Brick, cast stone, curtain wall

The new 321,000-square-foot Ambulatory Care Center for the University of Rochester's Strong Memorial Hospital consists of a consolidated medical center entrance (Access Center), an Ambulatory Care Building, improved access roadways, and a 1,200-car parking garage.

The Access Center creates a new paradigm for patient reception, integrating business, medical records, nursing, laboratory, and radiology functions for seamless reception of both inpatients and outpatients. Designed for the movement of up to 15,000 patients and visitors a day, the Access Center provides clearly defined entries and pathways that encourage quick and orderly movement, provide clear orientation, and reduce stress, confusion and anxiety.

The patient-focused character of the project is further emphasized through the integration of daylight and orientation to nature. The Ambulatory Care Building incorporates modular planning for the efficient delivery of clinical care and easy remodeling with minimal disruption to the delivery of care.

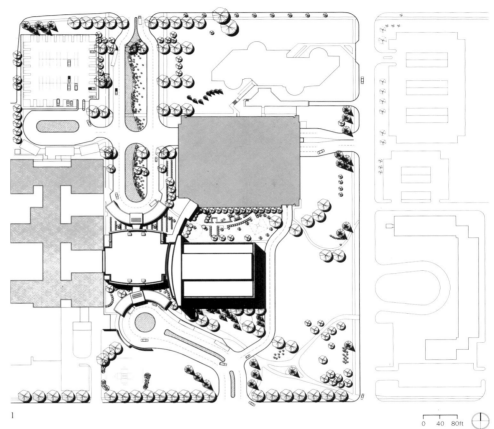

1

0 40 80ft

2

3

1   Site plan
2   South lobby
3   Ambulatory Care Building

RESEARCH

Battelle Memorial Institute Northwest Technical Research Center (Richland Campus)

Design/Completion 1966/1976 (Master Plan), 1966/1967 (Phase I),
1968/1969 (Phase II), 1968/1970 (Phase III), 1974/1976 (Phase IV)
Richland, Washington
Battelle Memorial Institute Pacific Northwest Laboratories
373,000 square feet total
Diverse precast concrete elements, stucco, glass, aluminum

Under continuous phased development from 1966 to 1976, Battelle Northwest was designed to accommodate advanced research over a broad spectrum of scientific investigation.

Located in a semi-arid area along the Columbia River, the building is surrounded by irrigated fields of alfalfa. The interior courtyard pool serves as an organizing device for the campus and as an evaporative cooler for the mechanical system. The Battelle campus was named "Laboratory of the Year" in 1968 by *Industrial Research and Development* magazine.

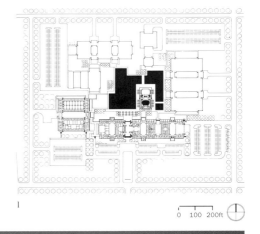

1

2

1   Site plan
2   Central reflecting and cooling pond
3   Main entrance
4   Large autoclave

3

4

Battelle Memorial Institute Seattle Conference Center

Design/Completion 1968/1969 (Phase I), 1968/1971 (Phase II)
Seattle, Washington
Battelle Memorial Institute Northwest Laboratories
60,222 gross square feet over 18 acres of a 20-acre site
Dark-stained cedar

Located in a residential district, the Battelle Seattle Conference Center was designed as an international seminar and research facility for visiting scholars and scientists.

A secluded and tranquil environment was created in the midst of an urban neighborhood by reclaiming 18 acres of tree-lined swamp and departing from the rigid grid pattern of the adjacent suburb. As Battelle's self-proclaimed "tungsten tower," the complex is an internally focused hermitage, constructed of dark-stained cedar and situated in a natural basin about 20 feet below the surrounding land.

With the sheltering roofs of its focal courtyard and its quiet lake (once a part of a larger nearby lake), the center epitomizes the Pacific Northwest's architectural blending of Scandinavian and Japanese traditions. This was the world's first application of weathering steel (Corten) as a roofing material.

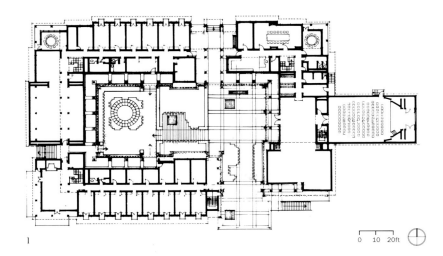

1

0   10   20ft

2

1   Floor plan, seminar building
2   Staff offices
3   Dining facility
4   Courtyard, seminar building

3

4

Salk Institute Cancer Research Animal Facility Addition

Design/Completion 1976/1978
La Jolla, California
Salk Institute for Biological Studies
23,000 gross square feet
Concrete

At the urging of the architect, this major addition to one of the nation's most prominent research institutes—and most beloved of Louis Kahn's architectural landmarks—was sited below grade along the south façade of the existing building. Only the service court, the raised lawn, surrounding perimeter walls, and the twin towers at the southeast corner (often perceived as part of the original structure) evidence this respectful addition to one of the century's most revered edifices.

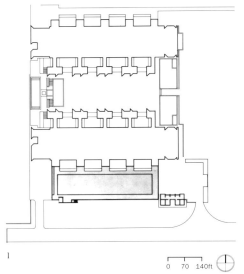

1

0   70   140ft

2

3

1 Site plan
2 View from the southwest showing lawn over the new edition
3 Air intake and exhaust towers
4 Floor plan
5 View from roof of new addition with new towers and walls on right

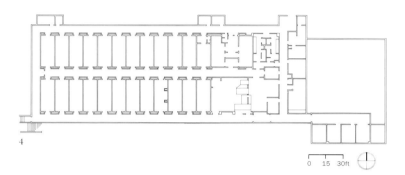

4

0   15   30ft

5

University of Washington Fluke Hall
(Washington Technology Center)

Design/Completion 1984/1990
Seattle, Washington
University of Washington
60,000 square feet
Masonry (brick and concrete) and metal-clad structures

A "technology transfer" facility for a broad
range of research activities, Fluke Hall is a
cooperative effort between the university
and industry conducted by the
Washington Technology Center, a
consortium specializing in the fields
of microelectronics, biotechnology,
manufacturing engineering, computer
science, and advanced materials. Its
mission is to accelerate the spread of
research and ideas from laboratory to
marketplace by providing a campus home
for industry researchers to work closely
with academic researchers.

Fluke Hall represents a direct response
to site and programmatic requirements,
articulating WTC's three functional
elements: lab, support, and service/
circulation. Sited on a steep slope
descending to the flat eastern edge
of the campus, the 60,000-square-foot hall
reflects both the collegiate Gothic
architecture of the parent university and
the industrial character of the university's
eastern boundary.

Continued

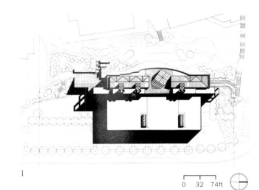

1

0   32   74ft

2

154

1 Site plan
2 View of west elevation looking southeast
3 View from the southwest showing support areas,
   central circulation, and research area
4 First floor
5 Second floor
6 Third floor

3

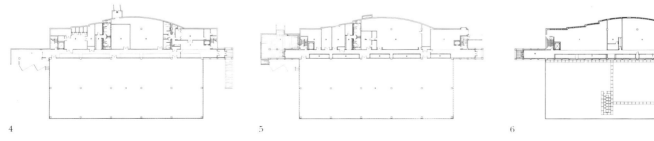

4   5   6

0   20 40ft

Administrative and support areas are housed in a two-story masonry structure set into the sloping hillside. Lab space resides on the flat lower portion of the site in a two-story metal-clad building that reflects its industrial purpose and relates to industrial support activities of the campus. A concrete spine of circulation corridors and ductwork for mechanical systems joins the two wings. Extending the full three-story height of the complex, this open, rectangular slot features clerestory windows that fill the space with light and accent enormous stainless steel air ducts and other services serving the laboratory spaces.

8

9

7   Central circulation corridor
8   Rooftop conference pavilion and mechanical
    enclosure
9   Flexible research space with built-in floor and
    ceiling services

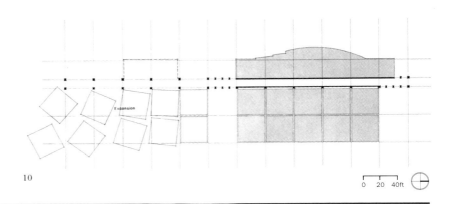

10

0 20 40ft

11

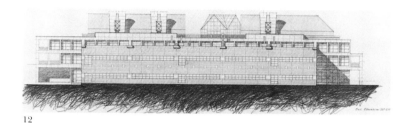

12

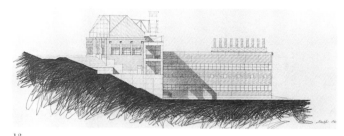

13

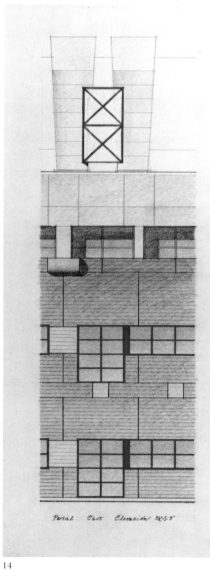

14

15

University of California Davis Medical Center, Medical Research Buildings I & II

Design/Completion 1988/1992
Sacramento, California
University of California, Davis Medical Center
MRB I: 32,600 square feet
MRB II: 44,400 square feet

NBBJ's master plan for UC Davis Medical Center's 20-acre Instruction and Research Zone included establishment of building sites, phased construction strategies, and designation of an academic quad and urban wildlife preserve. Two buildings for biomedical and clinical research were subsequently designed and constructed.

The twin structures are designed as flexible environments fostering both collaborative effort and private reflection. A traditional collegiate image is reinforced with brick, exhaust chimneys, and punched openings. The Central Valley's agricultural ties are reflected in simple shapes, strong roof profiles, and deep shade. The industrial quality of research is emphasized by steel tracery elements and a factory curtain wall.

1

2

1 Elevation study
2 Master plan showing new campus green and ultimate development
3 Medical research building with office block in foreground and laboratories beyond
4 Typical floor plan
5 Roof detail

3

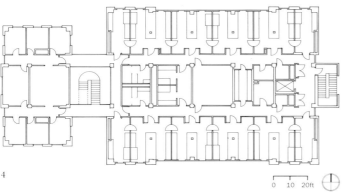

4

0 10 20ft

5

University of California Davis Medical Center, Medical Research Buildings I & II 161

ZymoGenetics New Corporate Headquarters

Design/Completion 1992/1994
Seattle, Washington
ZymoGenetics/The Koll Company
174,346 square feet
Reinforced concrete and brick exterior renovation and total new interior
construction

Built in four phases between 1911 and 1922, Seattle's historic Lake Union Steam Plant became a large, open trapezoidal concrete shell perched at the water's edge on 2,000 original-growth timber pilings, and made still more prominent with seven 60-foot smokestacks and banks of tall, slender windows facing the lake. After 72 years of duty, the plant was closed, and designated a historic landmark in 1989. ZymoGenetics, a rapidly growing biotechnology firm, selected the unused plant in 1992 as its corporate headquarters and main laboratory.

The original plant's main floor comprised one vast room with 40-foot-high ceilings to hold massive boilers, generators, turbines, and relay and support conduits—23 million pounds of equipment and materials that had to be removed at the beginning of reconstruction. Tremendous foundation floors, battered and scarred by the heavy equipment, were removed, the first floor slab replaced and the remaining space subdivided into functional floors for research.

Continued

1

1   View from the west
2   Typical laboratory floor plan
3   Typical laboratory
4   Central elevator core

2

0 10 20ft

3

4

Located within a mile of downtown Seattle, the resulting complex provides 113,000 square feet of office and research space on five floors, and two levels of underground parking. While the distinctive external appearance of the original facility has been retained, a comprehensive internal transformation has been achieved, from open shell housing electric generating equipment to versatile and sophisticated administrative offices and research laboratories.

5

6

5   View from the north
6   Central stair vignette

University of Wyoming Environmental Simulation Facility

Design/Completion 1995/1996
Laramie, Wyoming
University of Wyoming Center for Environmental Simulation Studies
71,916 gross square feet (37,418 net square feet)
Split and ground-faced exposed and precast concrete masonry,
metal roofing, clear and frit glass, painted metal

The Environmental Simulation Facility (ESF) establishes a national center for advanced research in environmental and natural resources and the effects of pollution such as oil spills and toxic waste storage. The first facility to offer such a breadth of capabilities, ESF simulates the interaction of water, soil, plants, and climate at scales representative of natural conditions using sophisticated lysimeters.

The three-story building continues the development of a northeastern corner of the University of Wyoming campus designated as a scientific research and development zone that includes the prominent Centennial Complex and the Animal Science and Molecular Biology Building. Constructed of precast and exposed concrete, and finished in brick, clear and frit glass, and painted metal roofing, ESF combines collegiate and industrial design elements.

1

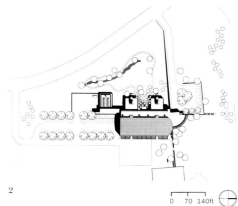

2

0   70   140ft

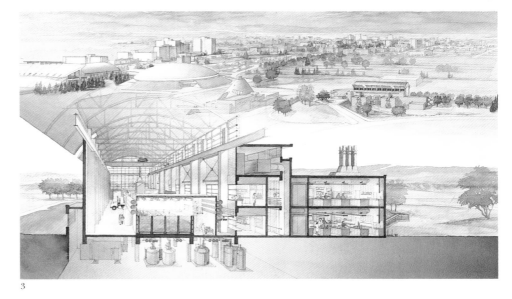

3

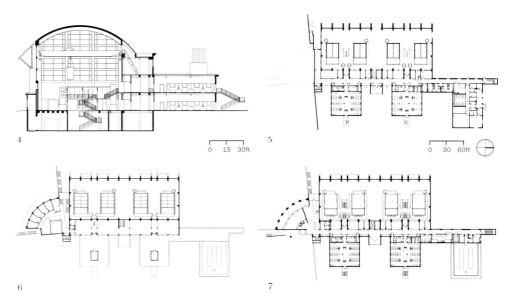

4

0   15   30ft

5

0   30   60ft

6

7

1   View of model looking northeast
2   Site plan
3   Artist's sectional perspective
4   Transverse section
5   First floor plan
6   Third floor plan
7   Second floor plan (main entrance)

EDUCATION

Washington State University, Fine Arts Building

Design/Completion 1968/1971
Pullman, Washington
Washington State University
96,024 square feet
Brick infill panels set in sandblasted exposed concrete frame

Designed as a multi-story linear loft structure to accommodate the departments of Architecture, Fine Arts, Landscape Architecture, Interior Design, and Industrial Design, the building follows the steeply sloping site with studios on the upper levels and parking on the lower levels.

A clerestory-lit pedestrian street with open stairs, balconies, lounges, and display areas provides a dynamic setting for the interplay of activities. The opening of the studio spaces to the pedestrian street provides a source of natural light.

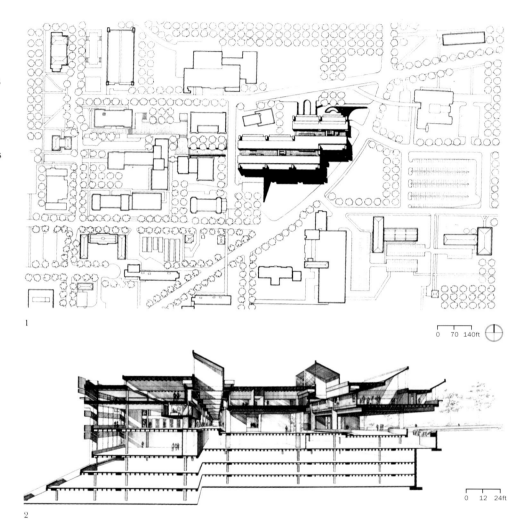

1

0 70 140ft

2

0 12 24ft

1   Site plan
2   Sectional perspective
3   View from the southeast
4   Entry level
5   Studio level
6   Parking/classroom level

3

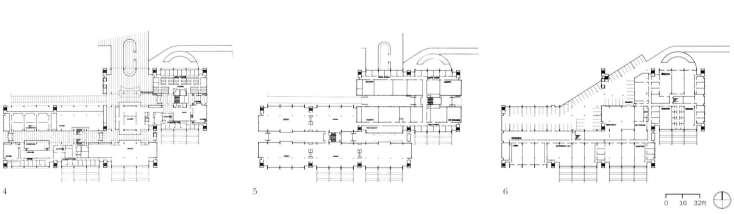

4   5   6

0 16 32ft

Worthington Kilbourne High School

Design/Completion 1989/1991
Worthington, Ohio
Worthington School District
272,000 square feet
Steel structure, exterior brick on block, interior block demountable
partitions

Pitched roofs, carefully detailed brick, and residentially scaled windows contribute to an architectural expression that is compatible with the surrounding residential neighborhood and conveys the importance assigned education in the Worthington community. The spanning of a site ravine is viewed by the staff as a metaphor for their mission of providing an educational bridge from childhood to adulthood, while an open walkway beneath the classroom-bridge allows evening football crowds to cross without compromising school security.

Worthington Kilbourne High School serves 1,500 students and includes a 13,000-square-foot library, a 750-seat auditorium, a 2,000-seat gymnasium, and 65 classrooms and laboratories.

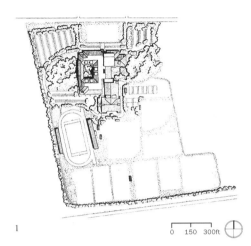

1

0   150 300ft

2

1   Site plan
2   Classroom bridge
3   Courtyard
4   First floor plan
5   Second floor plan
6   Bridge with open walkway
7   Gymnasium, view from the east

3

6

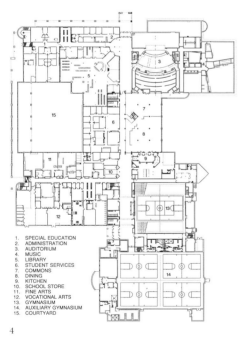

1. SPECIAL EDUCATION
2. ADMINISTRATION
3. AUDITORIUM
4. MUSIC
5. LIBRARY
6. STUDENT SERVICES
7. COMMONS
8. DINING
9. KITCHEN
10. SCHOOL STORE
11. FINE ARTS
12. VOCATIONAL ARTS
13. GYMNASIUM
14. AUXILIARY GYMNASIUM
15. COURTYARD

4

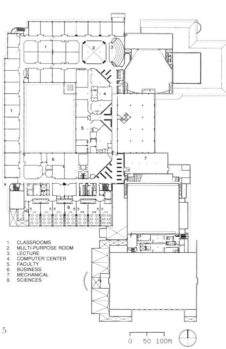

1. CLASSROOMS
2. MULTI-PURPOSE ROOM
3. LECTURE
4. COMPUTER CENTER
5. FACULTY
6. BUSINESS
7. MECHANICAL
8. SCIENCES

5

0   50   100ft

7

Canyon View Elementary School

Design/Completion 1984/1989
Tucson, Arizona
Catalina Foothills School District
54,160 square feet over 11 structures
Concrete block with brick coping

Straddling a natural arroyo in the rugged foothills of the Catalina Mountains, and close to Sabino Canyon National Monument and a new low-density development, Canyon View Elementary comprises 11 desert-hued buildings constructed of concrete block with brick coping. A pedestrian bridge spans the arroyo as the central component of a network of covered walkways in galvanized steel painted vibrant blue. As well as directing circulation and linking distinct sections of the campus, the canopies also provide deep shade from the intense Arizona sun.

Dramatic views of the landscape, dotted with saguaro cactus and paloverde, are preserved with the open corridor plan, large windows, and broad play areas. The library faces the mountains to the north, and includes a windowed reading nook that looks out into the arroyo.

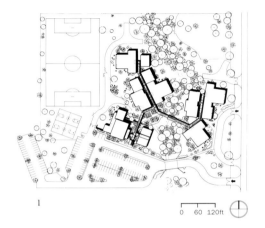

1

2

3

1   Site plan
2   Arroyo bridge from the southeast
3   Interior court
4   Vignette with saguaro cactus
5   Floor plan
6   Looking northeast toward Catolina Mountains

4

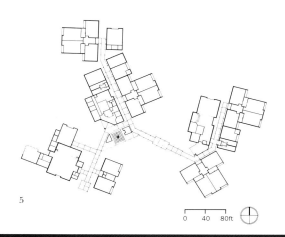

5

0   40   80ft

6

DeMiguel Elementary School

Design/Completion 1988/1990
Flagstaff, Arizona
Flagstaff School District
65,000 square feet
Brick, metal trim and roof

Sited amid a Ponderosa pine forest, DeMiguel Elementary School embraces its good fortune with a plan that simultaneously integrates and preserves the landscape.

The desire for a "clear and logical, but also dramatic and inviting" campus was achieved by following the site's steep contours, which both minimized construction cuts and fills and maintained stands of trees. The sloping site is accommodated by a two-tiered circulation spine, along which all classrooms are arrayed. A continuous south-facing clerestory along the spine serves both to frame forest views and to act as a passive solar heater during the often severe Flagstaff winters.

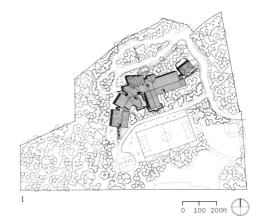

1

0 100 200ft

2

1 Site plan
2 View looking north
3 Academic piazza, south side
4 Central circulation area with gym beyond
5 Floor plans

3

4

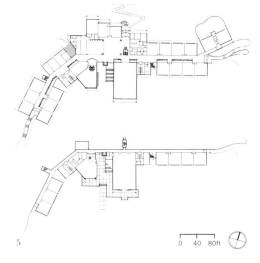

5

0 40 80ft

Howard E. LeFevre Hall, Central Ohio Technical College/Ohio State University at Newark

Design/Completion 1990/1993
Newark, Ohio
Central Ohio Technical College/Ohio State University at Newark
55,000 gross square feet
Rough concrete masonry with brick protrusions and metallic wall panels

Howard E. LeFevre Hall brings together in one building classes in electronics and industrial technology and classes in dance, drama, music, and the fine arts. It serves as a focal point for Central Ohio Technical College, a small commuter branch campus of the Ohio State University.

This "right brain/left brain" structure expresses both technical and artistic programs while responding to the equally dichotomous site, which rests along the western edge of the foothills of eastern Ohio and marks the beginning of the Midwestern plains. These topographical changes find overt reference in the building's slow rise from single-story western volume to two-story eastern volume. The dichotomy finds further expression in the exterior mechanical louvers, which cant away from the wall in the way a painting hangs. End-grained wood floors, revered by artists and dancers for their suppleness and warmth and favored by industrialists for their loading capacity and durability, are used on the interior.

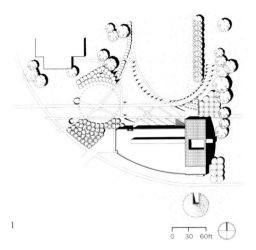

1

2

1 Site plan
2 Entrance
3 Exterior wall detail
4 Exterior wall at stair
5 First floor
6 Second floor

3

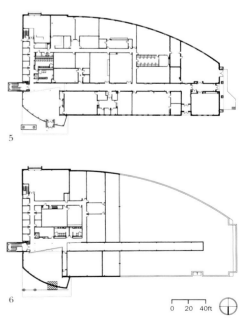

5

6

0 20 40ft

4

7

7　Central corridor
8　View from the south

8

Harold M. Nestor Academic Center

Design/Completion 1992/1993
Columbus, Ohio
Columbus State Community College
128,000 square feet (5 stories)
Steel frame
Iron spot beige and patterned red brick veneer,
polished black granite, corrugated metal

The curving facade of Nestor Academic
Center becomes the new urban face of
Columbus State Community College,
serves as a gateway to the campus, and
encloses its main quadrangle.

The Center comprises 48 classrooms,
9 laboratories, 80 faculty offices, a seminar
center, conference and music rooms, and
a 375 seat auditorium.

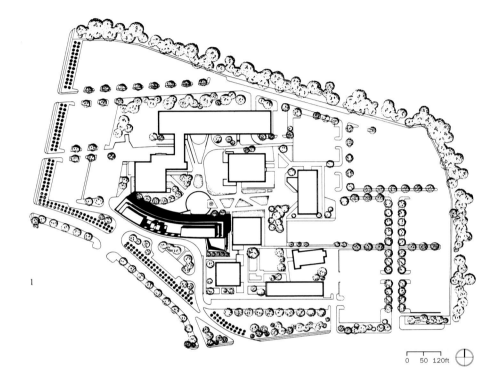

1

0   50   120ft

2

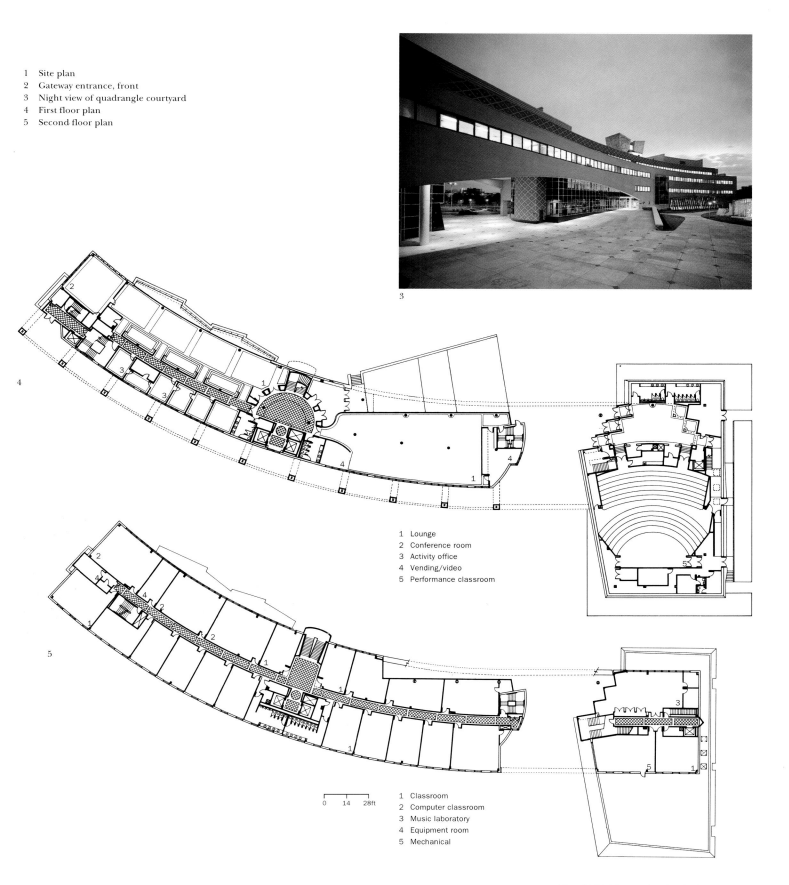

1 Site plan
2 Gateway entrance, front
3 Night view of quadrangle courtyard
4 First floor plan
5 Second floor plan

3

4

1 Lounge
2 Conference room
3 Activity office
4 Vending/video
5 Performance classroom

5

0   14   28ft

1 Classroom
2 Computer classroom
3 Music laboratory
4 Equipment room
5 Mechanical

Center Hall (University of California San Diego Classroom Building I)

Design/Completion 1993/1995
San Diego, California
University of California, San Diego
63,580 square feet
Split-faced concrete block, stucco, and steel

Center Hall houses 16 general assignment classrooms and lecture halls with combinations of 30, 80, 120, 150, 200, and 300 seats for a total seating capacity of 2,000. The new facility forms two adjacent sides of a proposed new quadrangle, and includes computer labs, seminar rooms, office and tutoring space for the Office of Academic Support and Instructional Services (OASIS), and video production and editing labs for the Center for Teaching Development (CTD).

These popular functions, housed together in this centrally sited building, create an academic and functional centerpiece for the university.

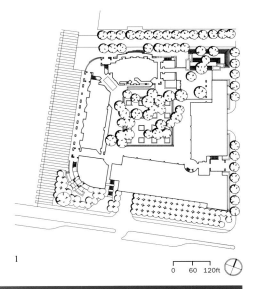

1

0   60   120ft

2

1   Site plan
2   Primary entrance, northwest corner
3   View of north wing looking southwest

3

4

5

4 Typical classroom/lecture hall
5 Detail at stair
6 View of west wing looking southeast
7 First floor
8 Second floor
9 Third floor

6

7

8

9

0   30   60ft

Shanghai American School

Design/Completion 1995/1997
Shanghai, People's Republic of China
Shanghai American School
94,090 square meters (1.01 million square feet)
Clay tile roof, stucco wall, curtain wall for exterior, cast concrete
structure, cast stone used as wainscot

The Shanghai American School offers
Western-accredited education from
kindergarten through high school to
students with English as either the primary
or secondary language. The desire for
a campus that conforms to Western
standards of education and construction
while capturing the unique qualities of
China deeply influenced the design.

Rather than copying traditional Chinese
architectural forms, the design establishes
a modern expression appropriate to China
and the educational nature of the campus.
Inspired by the principles and philosophy
of Chinese garden design, the Shanghai
American School extends learning beyond
the classroom to encompass the entire
physical setting of the campus. At each
step students are invited, in a gentle
way, to learn something about the world
around them. Embracing the qualities
of scholar, poet, and painter, the campus
balances the Confucian love of order with
the Taoist love of nature in a descriptive
comparison of virtues.

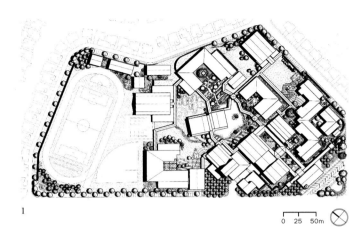

1

2

1   Site plan
2   Aerial perspective
3   Courtyard of Three Friends
4   Courtyard of Everlasting Stability
5   Garden of Literature
6   Garden of Science and Geometry
7   Media Center
8   Campus commons

3

4

5

6

7

8

Ohio Wesleyan University, The James A. Young Memorial Walk (JAYwalk)

Design/Completion 1991/1994
Delaware, Ohio
Ohio Wesleyan University
63,580 square feet
Stone pavers, concrete pavers, poured-in-place concrete, sandstone walls, stainless steel signage

The James A. Young Memorial Walk—a central spine connecting academic and social elements of college life—exemplifies liberal arts ideals. The uninterrupted, handicapped-accessible path links educational, recreational, residential, and leisure buildings in a winding east-to-west concourse between Sandusky and Washington streets.

Beautifully landscaped outdoor rooms, including botanical plantings and a Shakespearean garden, are designed to relate to adjacent buildings and provide space for lectures, readings, and performances. Seats, benches, steps, and patio walls throughout the site invite relaxation, reflection, and gathering.

1

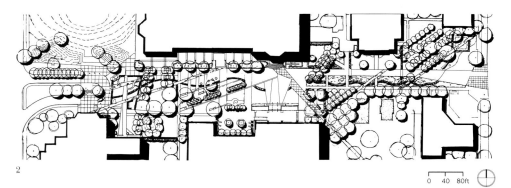

2

0   40   80ft

3

1   Looking southwest at entrance to Shakespearean garden
2   Site plan
3   Dining commons looking northeast

California Maritime Academy

Design/Completion 1997/1999
Vallejo, California
California Maritime Academy
18,000 square feet
Steel and cast-in-place concrete
Stainless steel ribbed wall panel exterior skin

Located at the entrance to Carquinez Strait, the California Maritime Academy prepares young cadets for careers in the merchant marine on a small site at the water's edge. Lack of an available flat site for building, together with some critical academic adjacencies, have placed this new laboratory facility on the edge of a very steep hill.

The building is conceived of as a single two-story box, manipulated to clarify the architectural definition of the campus. The north end of the building is aligned with the geometry of the central campus buildings while the computer lab and learning center face the nearby library.

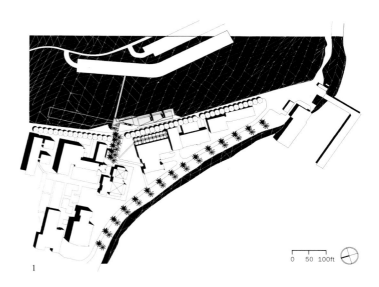

1

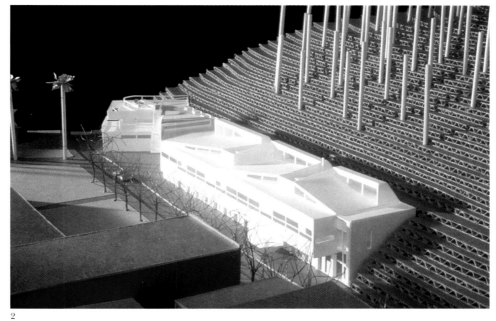

2

1   Site plan
2   Model view looking northeast

SPORTS & ENTERTAINMENT

Bagley Wright Theater

Design/Completion 1981/1983
Seattle, Washington
City of Seattle/Seattle Center
9-story equivalent: 71,571 gross square feet
Steel
Horizontal prefabricated stucco skin with aluminum banding

The 864-seat Bagley Wright Theater has been acclaimed as being in "the ranks of the best theater buildings in the country" by the *Christian Science Monitor.* That quality derives from several special factors, including intimacy of seating and diversity of function.

A 500-seat orchestra level with a 364-seat, seven-row balcony insures no seat is further than 18 rows (55 feet) from the theater's 48-foot deep by 96-foot wide proscenium stage. Guided by Seattle Repertory Theater's administrative and creative directors, the design specifically incorporates superior sightlines and acoustics: all seats are within the actors' vision at all times and, crafted "for the spoken word," the house allows actors to be heard with utmost subtlety and clarity.

The central performance and audience space, together with lobby and circulation areas, comprises only a quarter of the whole facility, the remainder housing the support and rehearsal spaces necessary to realize quality productions.

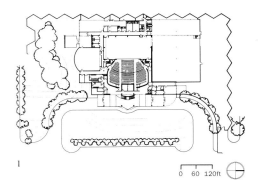

1

0   60   120ft

2

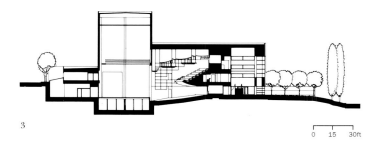

3

0   15   30ft

1   Site plan
2   View from the northeast
3   Transverse section
4   View from the northeast in the evening
5   Lobby
6   Lobby bar

4

5

6

Clark State Community College Performing Arts Center

Design/Completion 1990/1993
Springfield, Ohio
Clark State Community College
85,983 gross square feet
Steel
Brick

Clark State's Performing Arts Center is located in downtown Springfield to serve as both theater for the university's drama department and performance venue for the town, with college and public entrances facing different main thoroughfares. The center comprises the 1,500-seat multi-purpose Kuss Auditorium; a 250-seat studio theater for instruction, rehearsal, and more intimate performances; four classrooms; faculty offices; community rooms accommodating 125; and back-of-house support areas.

Simple details and inexpensive materials addressed budgetary limitations and assured relative elegance. A system of variable acoustics concealed above the ceiling and high side walls insures the building's multi-use potential. The result is a lean but vibrant facility suitable for theatrical and musical performances ranging from full plays to one-actor shows, and from bands to symphonies.

1

1   Main theater entrance
2   First floor plan
3   Lower balcony plan
4   Upper balcony plan
5   View of main theater from stage

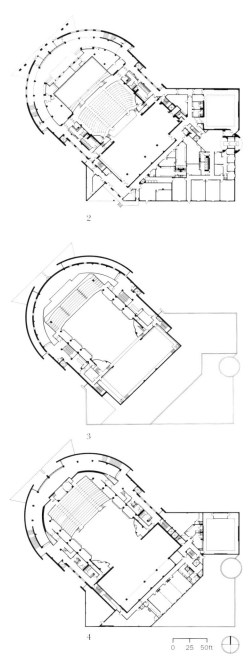

2

3

4

0 25 50ft

5

KeyArena

Design/Completion 1992/1995
Seattle, Washington
Seattle Center
17,000-seat arena
Concrete; aluminum roof; steel truss system structure above main floor
line; glass window wall partially replacing the existing glass window wall
and steel window wall frame; concrete block masonry in a number of
different configurations both ground faced and spectra glazed; painted
gypsum wallboard walls; suites are wood-trimmed and carpeted

Lauded by the Seattle press as "recycling
on a grand scale," the KeyArena project
reclaimed the desultory and "economically
obsolete" Seattle Center Coliseum as an
inviting and superbly functional basketball
pavilion for half the cost of a new arena.
The result is a 17,000-seat venue (formerly
14,000) with superior sight lines,
remarkable intimacy, and 58 luxury suites,
accomplished by demolishing the interior
and excavating 35 feet deeper into the
earth.

The existing leaky, cable-suspended roof
was replaced, but its graceful contours
were recreated economically with curved
steel trusses at the four corner locations
allowing all other framing members to
be straight steel sections.

*"If you are a stone basketball fan and want the
optimum basketball experience, there's no place like
KeyArena. The sight lines, presentation and
atmosphere at the Key may be unrivaled
in the NBA."*
Glenn Nelson, Sports Writer

1

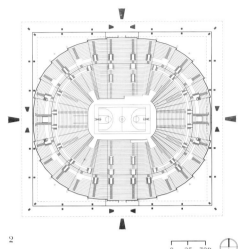

2

0 35 70ft

3

1   Construction photograph with cable-suspended
    roof removed
2   Floor plan after renovation
3   West entrance
4   Configured for basketball
5   Transverse section before (left) and after (right)
    renovation
6   Photo of west entrance taken from level of original
    arena floor

4

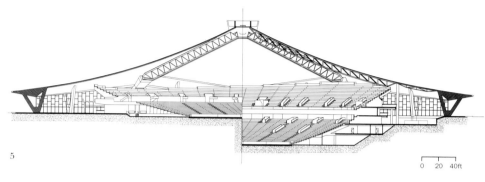

5

0 20 40ft

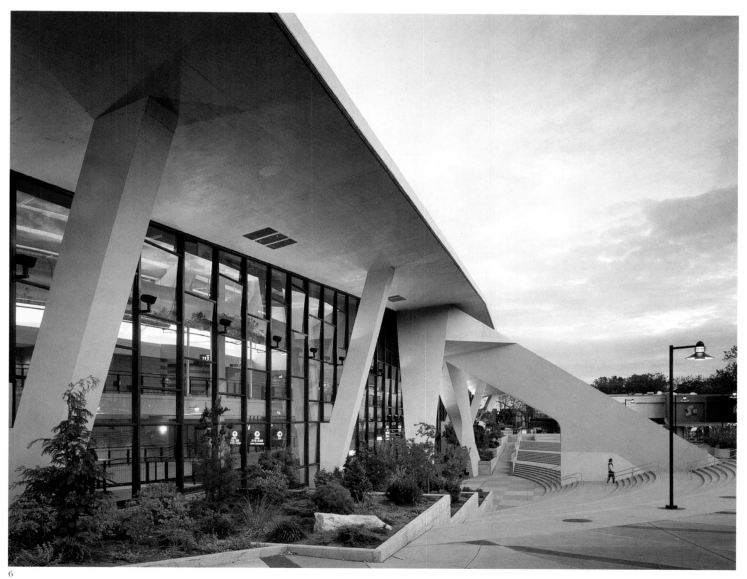

6

New Pacific Northwest Baseball Park

Design/Completion 1995/1999
Seattle, Washington
Public Facilities District
45,000-seat stadium
Brick, stone, precast concrete, exposed structural steel

Seattle's New Pacific Northwest Baseball Park mixes nostalgia for the grand fields of baseball's heyday with demands for contemporary hospitality and services. Its mostly brick façade and curved entry behind home plate refer directly to such great arenas as Ebbett's Field, Yankee Stadium, and the Polo Grounds, while responding to dual contextual forces: Seattle's historic Pioneer Square district and the nearby Port of Seattle industrial core with its waterfront docks and giant steel cranes.

The 10-acre, 650-foot-span retractable canopy roof is stacked over the adjacent railroad tracks, recalling both the great 19th century steel-trussed train stations and the waterfront cranes nearby. Gliding over the playing field on steel rails, the roof insures cozy cover from Seattle's gloomy bouts of rain, and stacks to the east away from the stands for those golden days of summer.

Continued

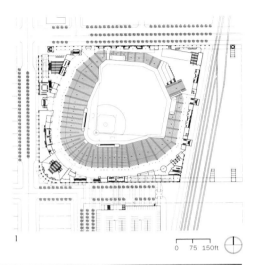

1   Site plan
2   View from the northwest with roof closed
3   Northwest entrance
4   Cross-sectional model
5   Section at south wall, infield
6   Section at north wall, outfield bleachers

3

4

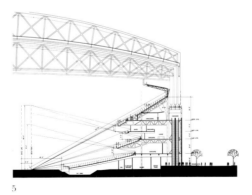

5

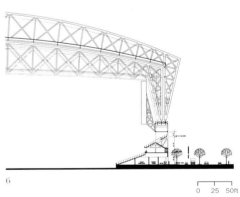

6

0   25   50ft

Seating 45,000, the park will include deluxe and party suites, administrative offices for the Seattle Mariners, a stadium club, restaurants, and state-of-the-art clubhouses—all facing a natural grass field. Fans in the park's upper levels will enjoy vistas of downtown and Pioneer Square, Elliott Bay, the Olympic Mountains, and Mt Rainier.

7

8

0 25 50ft

9

7 East–west section with roof closed
8 East–west section with roof open
9 View from the northwest with roof open

R.H. Johnson Memorial Stadium/Doubleday Field at US Military Academy, West Point

Design 1996
West Point, New York
The Doubleday Society/The United States Military Academy
850-seat stadium
Rough granite with limestone accents

Named for Abner Doubleday (a 1842 West Point graduate best known as the father of modern baseball), Doubleday Field has been home plate for the army team since 1902. When plans were announced to move play to another site, academy alumni and former team members formed the Doubleday Society to sponsor a permanent structure.

Sited on "The Plain"—West Point's historic parade grounds—the field is a landmark protected by the New York State Historic Preservation Office. Any alteration required that agency's approval. A design strategy of "unobtrusive intervention" satisfied both preservation and facility requirements. The structure's low profile minimizes its visibility from The Plain, while its façade of rough granite with limestone accents recalls materials of adjacent campus buildings. The new stadium seats 850 and includes a clubhouse, coaching offices, home and visiting team locker rooms, and public restrooms.

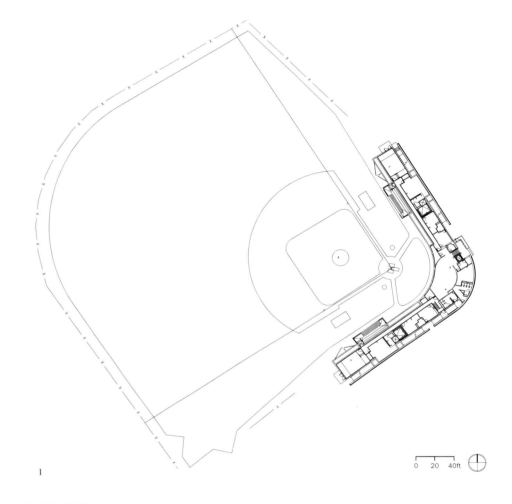

1

0 20 40ft

2

1 Plan view
2 Perspective view

Miller Park

Design/Completion 1995/2000
Milwaukee, Wisconsin
42,000-seat stadium
Brick, stone, precast concrete, and exposed structural steel
Winning competition entry

Joining classic turn-of-the-century stadium design with modern state-of-the-art technology, Miller Park offers the best of all worlds: outdoor baseball on natural turf and a fully retractable roof to protect against inclement weather.

The 42,500-seat stadium includes 75 skyboxes and 3,000 club seats, a center field scoreboard with massive video display, plus an exterior video display tower with digital message board. The fan-shaped roof opens or closes in five minutes.

1

0   150 300ft

2

1   Site plan
2   Home plate entrance with roof retracted
3   Aerial view with roof retracted
4   Towers at VIP entrance
5   Aerial view with roof closed
6–8 Study sketches

3

4

5

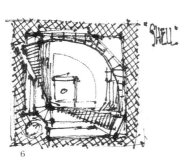

6

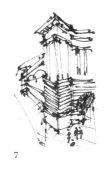

7

8

Charles J. Ping Student Recreation Center, Ohio University

Design/Completion 1992/1995
Athens, Ohio
Ohio University
172,000 square feet
Steel structure
Brick, glazed aluminum curtain wall, stucco exterior

Overlooking the Hocking River, the 172,000-square-foot Charles J. Ping Student Recreation Center includes five hardwood courts for basketball and volleyball; eight enclosed courts for racquetball, volleyball, and squash; two multi-purposes courts with synthetic floors; a multi-use martial/combative arts room; aerobic and fitness areas; an elevated jogging and walking track; a 36-foot climbing wall; and a field for soccer and field hockey. Small child care and game areas, meeting and locker rooms, and a lounge complete the facility.

In keeping with the campus tradition of Georgian architecture, the Ping Center incorporates punched and arched windows, and flat and articulated masonry walls with large glazed areas.

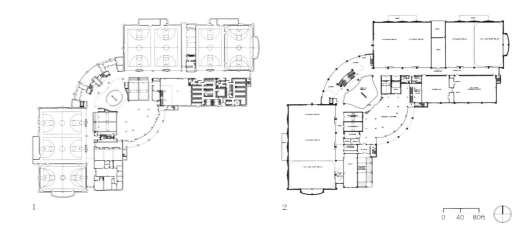

1   2

0   40   80ft

3

1   First floor plan
2   Second floor plan
3   View of student patio
4   View from the south
5   View from the southeast
6   Main lobby climbing wall

4

6

5

Cincinnati Bengals New NFL Stadium Study

Design 1996
Cincinnati, Ohio
70,000-seat stadium

Unlike many new generation stadia, which shroud their structures in masonry skins recalling an earlier era, the structure in this proposal remains exposed. Variety and interest are achieved by development and expression of the non-uniform bowl, a result of carefully studied fan viewing preferences. The cantilevered fabric roof protects as many fans as possible while still achieving an open feel. The translucent material serves as a screen for projected images ranging from team logos and advertisements to community messages.

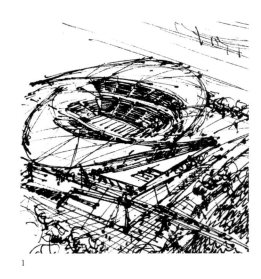

1

2

1   Study sketch
2   View from the Ohio River
3   Aerial view showing relationship to existing
    riverfront stadium

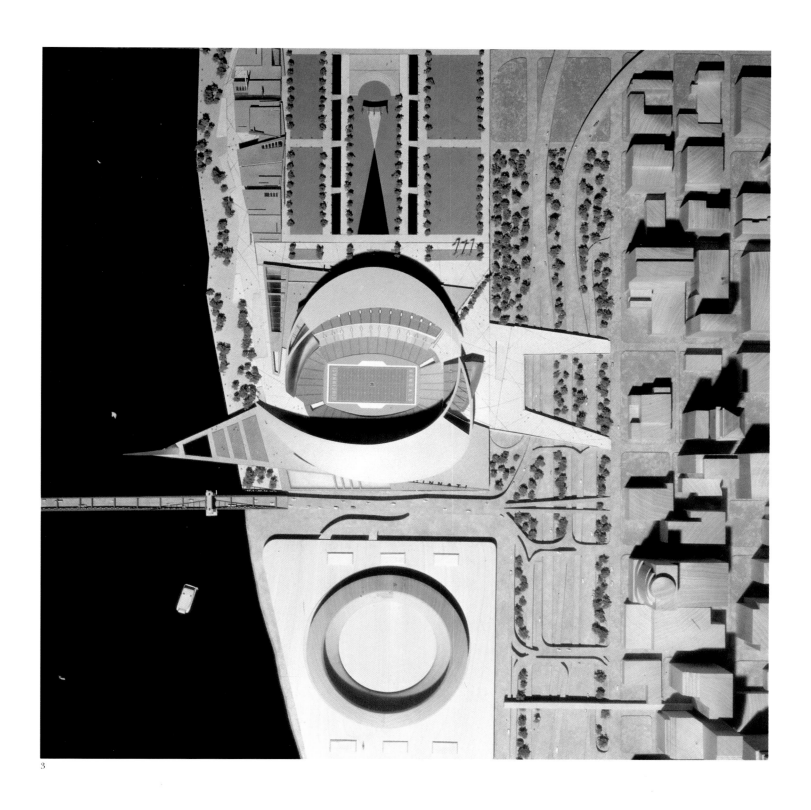

3

RETAIL & GRAPHIC DESIGN

Pasta & Co.

Design/Completion 1986/1987
Seattle, Washington
Pasta & Co.
2,500 square feet
Marble, stainless steel, porcelain enamel

This gourmet food specialty store is located in a pavilion at the base of a high-rise building in Seattle's central business district.

Dine-in, take-out, lunch delivery, and gourmet food areas are effectively and attractively arranged in this small prototype store. The architects provided space planning, graphic design, merchandising, and interior design services.

1

2

1 View from the pedestrian concourse
2 Dine-in area with take-out counter

Polo/Ralph Lauren

Design 1993
Tannersville, Pennsylvania
Polo/Ralph Lauren Retail Corporation
6,700 square feet
Pine, concrete, steel

This was one of over 50 factory outlet stores designed for Polo/Ralph Lauren. Each store has a design character appropriate to its region in addition to conveying the Polo/Ralph Lauren lifestyle image.

1

1   Central atrium

Banana Republic, Coliseum Theater

Design/Completion 1993/1994
Seattle, Washington
Banana Republic and Martin Smith, Inc.
12,000 square feet
Terra cotta exterior restoration; interior renovation

A palatial movie theater on one of downtown Seattle's most prominent corners, the Coliseum Theater languished for years until NBBJ conducted an adaptive reuse feasibility study and assisted with a subsequent marketing plan to attract potential tenants.

Built in 1916, the Coliseum was designed by prominent Seattle architect B. Marcus Priteca as the first West Coast theater dedicated to motion pictures. The theater suffered with the rise of multi-plex cinemas and closed in 1985. Though its glazed white terra cotta Italian Renaissance façade had been listed in the National Register of Historic Places in 1977, many feared for the Coliseum's existence.

Banana Republic, a member of the Gap Inc. retail chain, recognized the building's character and potential, and in 1993 agreed to transform it into a 12,000-square-foot single-level flagship retail outlet for upmarket apparel.

1

2

1   Exterior view at entry
2   Window detail (restored)

Puget Consumers' Co-Op

Design/Completion 1995/1996
Seattle, Washington
Puget Consumers' Co-Op
15,000 square feet
Concrete floor, MDF, block, steel

Directional and merchandising strategies
were part of the design challenge of this
prototype store designed for the nation's
largest cooperatively owned natural and
organic food grocer. Located in one of
the city's older historic neighborhoods,
it is a very "green" (environmentally
responsible) building, in keeping with
the values of the owners and users.

1

2

3

1   Produce department
2   Delicatessen
3   Exterior view at entry

Gene Jaurez Salon

Design/Completion 1995/1996
Tacoma, Washington
Gene Jaurez
10,000 square feet
Pear wood, marble, maple floor, linoleum, paint

It is intended that salon customers find themselves transported out of their daily lives of work and family into an environment of beauty and calm.
It is a place of comfort and warmth, of pampering and luxury—an oasis of pleasure in a busy life.

The architectural forms, bold materials and colors of the reception and waiting areas invite customers from the mall into the salon where they are encouraged by the drama of the curving wood retail wall to purchase hair and beauty products. The hair design and technical salons are innovative and playful: over-sized diamond patterns on the walls, and large gold leaf frames filled with merchandise add whimsy and sparkle. The spa, which is the ultimate retreat, is preceded by a small reception/retail area that is distinct from the rest of the salon in its atmosphere of quiet luxury.

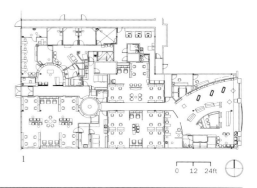

1   Floor plan
2   Check-out counter
3   Manicure salon
4   Styling salon
5   Entrance to spa

4

5

Mr. Rags

Design 1996
Bellevue Square, Bellevue, Washington
Lux Corporation
2,000 square feet
Concrete, hot rolled steel, 55 gallon drums, utility light sockets

Mr. Rags is a prototype design for an apparel store specializing in clothing and accessories for teenage boys and girls. Raw building materials are used in unusual applications to create a store with an attitude that matches that of its customers. Bare light bulbs that hang from a ceiling made from concrete reinforcing wire grid, flattened 55-gallon drums and sheets of hot rolled steel used as a wall cladding, exposed framing, and worn away painted concrete floors are combined with other raw materials to create an exciting and bold design that pushes the limits of traditional mall retail design. The store has received enthusiastic reviews from its customers and has resulted in increased sales and visibility for the retailer. The prototype design has been implemented in an aggressive roll-out program throughout the western states.

1

2

1 Accessory area
2 Storefront as seen from the mall

Pacific Place

Design/Completion 1994/1998
Seattle, Washington
Pine Street Development
975,000 gross square feet
Precast concrete, glass, metal

As the catalyst for the revitalization of Seattle's downtown retail core, the first phase of this two-block development includes a large urban entertainment complex. Consisting of 340,000 square feet of specialty retail and restaurants over a 1,200-car parking garage, the project is organized around a central skylit atrium and capped with an 11-screen General Cinema complex. The complex is linked to the newly renovated Nordstrom flagship store by a pedestrian skybridge, and its tenants include Sony, Williams-Sonoma Grande Cuisine and Pottery Barn, as well as Stars and Il Fornaio restaurants.

1

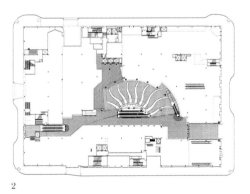

2

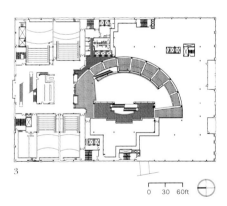

3

0   30   60ft

1   Model showing Pine Street (south) elevation
2   Upper street level plan
3   Fourth level, restaurant/cinema plan

NBBJ's award-winning graphic design department works with clients outside the realm of architecture as well as serving the needs of the firm. Todo Wraps restaurants and the Empty Space Theater are two such clients.

Todo Wraps restaurants combine international flavors in a high-energy atmosphere. To evoke a sense of fun, color and pattern are layered throughout the packaging. The international flavor concept is developed in a series of 16 "travel" stickers illustrating the origins of the food.

Posters must cut through the clutter of today's high-tech world, communicating the essentials with few words and immediate impact. Our ongoing work for the Empty Space Theater projects its reputation for presenting provocative, untried productions. A review of the early script and discussions with the director set the stage for the compelling imagery and engaging message that distinguish each poster.

1

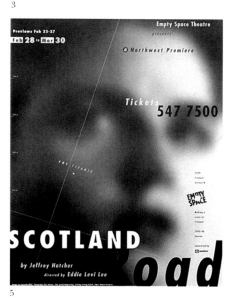

3

2

4

5

6

7

8

9

10

FIRM PROFILE

Timeline of Pivotal Events

1938–1943
Naramore and Brady, William J. Bain and Smith Carroll and Johanson associate on numerous projects for the US Navy at Bremerton culminating in the formation of NBBJ in 1943.

1943 NBBJ continues a long relationship with the Seattle School District begun by founding partner Floyd Naramore in the twenties.

1945 Nils Johanson, Director of Swedish Hospital, retains his nephew Perry Johanson for a small project that begins NBBJ's medical practice.

1949 NBBJ begins a long relationship with the Bellevue School District providing schools for baby-boomers.

1950 NBBJ moves from offices in the Smith Tower and Dexter Horton buildings into a new building at 904 7th Avenue in Seattle.

1950 The University of Washington asks NBBJ to design a new hospital and medical school campus, marking the beginning of a project that continues to involve the firm today.

1956 University Properties, operators of the 10-acre Metropolitan Tract owned by the University of Washington, retains NBBJ for a high-rise building and begins an ongoing relationship that produces much of Seattle's urban architecture.

1956 William Bain, Jr. returns from Cornell to join the firm.

1957 NBBJ wins Corregidor Island Competition memorializing the war in the Pacific.

1959 Donald Winkelmann, a recent Yale graduate and *Progressive Architecture* design award winner, joins the firm and begins work on a succession of award-winning projects.

1960 Partner Perry Johanson, a former classmate of Minoru Yamasaki, associates the firms for four major projects, including the US Pavilion at the 1962 World's Fair, now the Pacific Science Center.

1962 David Hoedemaker joins the firm following graduate school at Yale and an apprenticeship with Eero Saarinen.

1964 Founding partner "Doc" Brady dies.

1964 Business Space Design is created by Bob Messer, Bob Pope and Bob Burke to provide space planning and interior design to corporate tenants.

1965 The Naramore Foundation, benefiting architectural education, is created by Floyd Naramore.

1965 Jim Jonassen joins NBBJ following graduate school at Columbia.

1966 NBBJ selected for design of Battelle Memorial Institute's "think tank" in Seattle, resulting in a long-term, multi-project relationship.

1967 NBBJ opens Honolulu office.

1968 Two *Progressive Atchitecture* citations and three AIA design awards mark the beginning of NBBJ's design renaissance, now recognized by nearly 300 design awards.

1968 The 50-story Seattle First National Bank building (1001 4th Avenue), Seattle and NBBJ's first high-rise, wins praise from New York architectural critic Ada Louise Huxtable and an AIA Honor Award.

1971 Founding partner Floyd Naramore dies.

1973 NBBJ designs the 65,000-seat Kingdome from program through construction documents in six months. It has the world's longest span thin-shell concrete roof and was bid at $29.9 million (plus $10 million for the energy plant).

1974 After contracts with the original architect for the Federal Pavilion at Expo '74 in Spokane were terminated, NBBJ was asked to begin anew with construction to begin in three and a half months in order to meet the opening date. The design was approved in three weeks, construction began on schedule, and the completed, award-winning building appeared on the cover of *Progressive Architecture.*

1975 Management and Planning Services created to provide financial analysis, life-cycle costing and planning services.

1975 David Hoedemaker elected Managing Partner and CEO, succeeding Perry Johanson.

1975 NBBJ wins competition for Honolulu City Hall.

1976 NBBJ closes Honolulu office.

1976 Colleague firm network organized.

1976 NBBJ provides interior design and space planning services to the Kingdom of Saudi Arabia for 12 years.

1976 Friedl Böhm, an Austrian Fulbright Scholar, merges his young firm with NBBJ following an association on a major project in Columbus.

1976 Dave Haworth begins NBBJ's Management and Planning Services group providing economic analysis and financial feasibility in-house.

1977   The Mayo Clinic commissions NBBJ to design the world's largest surgical suite on the basis of a published article on a new surgical prototype designed by NBBJ for the Swedish Medical Center in Seattle.

1977   NBBJ merges with Maynard/Partch in Anchorage.

1979   Naramore Bain Brady and Johanson becomes The NBBJ Group.

1980   Principal role created.

1981   Founding partner Perry Johanson dies.

1981   NBBJ opens Palo Alto office, moving to San Francisco in 1988.

1983   Jim Jonassen assumes CEO responsibilities for the west coast.

1983   Friedl Böhm assumes CEO responsibilities for the east coast.

1983   Seattle and Columbus offices relocated to restored historic buildings.

1983   Merger with McClure Architecture in Raleigh.

1984   Merger creates NBBJ's Research Triangle Park, North Carolina office.

1985   Merger with Gresham/Larson, Tucson.

1985   Founding partner William J. Bain dies.

1987   Friedl Böhm elected Managing Partner.

1987   David Hoedemaker assumes newly created role of Partner in Charge of Design.

1987   John R. Pangrazio becomes a partner.

1988   David Zimmerman and Larry Helman become partners.

1989   Oregano, an annual two-week trip to a world capital for members of each NBBJ studio, inaugurated.

1989   Retail group starts with addition of Debbie DeGabrielle and James Adams.

1989   NBBJ opens Charleston office.

1990   NBBJ opens New York office, acquires the Rosenfield Partnership.

1991   The NBBJ Group becomes NBBJ.

1991   NBBJ opens Los Angeles office.

1991   Alan Patrick and staff, formerly of Patrick Plus, join NBBJ in Columbus.

1991   Scott Wyatt joins NBBJ, becomes a partner in 1994.

1992–present   NBBJ ranked number 1 in health care architecture by *Modern Healthcare* magazine.

1994   Neil Anderson becomes a partner

1994   NBBJ opens Tokyo office.

1994–present   NBBJ ranked second largest architectural firm in US, sixth in the world.

1995   Jack MacAllister joins NBBJ in San Francisco; becomes President of the California practice.

1995   Michael Hallmark, Ron Turner and Dan Meis join NBBJ forming NBBJ Sports and Entertainment in Los Angeles.

1995–96   NBBJ wins 13 of 17 competitions entered.

1996   Peter Pran joins NBBJ in Seattle.

1996   NBBJ named Best Company to Work For in Washington State by *Washington CEO* magazine.

1997   NBBJ Columbus moves into new offices at 1555 Lakeshore Drive.

1997   Friedl Böhm assumes the new role of Chairman, with responsibility for the firm's strategic direction and long-term performance.

1997   Jim Jonassen becomes Managing Partner with emphasis on the performance of the firm's studios and its practice world-wide.

1997   Neal Anderson becomes CEO of the firm's eastern offices, responsible, with the other eastern partners, for the performance of these offices.

1997   Scott Wyatt becomes CEO of the firm's western offices, responsible, with the other western partners, for the performance of these offices.

1997   Richard G. Buckley advances to partner

1997   Ted McCagg joins NBBJ as Principal and Director of Aviation/Transportation Services

Principals

Seattle
James D. Adams
Dorman D. Anderson
James E. Brinkley
Robert F. Bruckner
Stuart D. Charles
Richard F. Dallam
Donna F. Davis
Gary J. Edmonds
Dennis C. Forsyth
John F. Halleran
Cecile E. Haw
Michael A. Kreis
Bradley D. Leathley
Teresa N. Martin
Edward K. McCagg II
R. Steven McConnell
William J. Nichols
Peter C. Pran
William V. Sanford
John C. Savo
Rysia Suchecka
David H. Swain
K. Robert Swartz
Vincent Vergel de Dios
Jim R. Waymire
Richard L. Zieve

San Francisco
John E. MacAllister
Steven M. O'Brien
Howard I. Weiss

Los Angeles
Michael L. Hallmark
Daniel R. Meis
Ronald F. Turner

Columbus, OH
Michael L. Ball
Peter L. Bardwell
Alfred E. Berthold
Dennis A. Brandon
John H. Carr
Brian D. Connelly
Bernard J. Constantino
David J. Dahnke
Timothy M. Fishking
Ruth Gless
Robert Klie III
Gregory C. Mare
Richard H. Morse
R. Douglas Parris
Allen L. Patrick
Myron A. (Jack) Pettit
Daniel R. Pickett
James H. Schirtzinger
Fred E. Weingand

New York
Martha A. Burns
Pamela J. Jenkins

Research Triangle Park
Philip L. Szostak

In Recognition of the Contributions of Earlier Leaders
Floyd A. Naramore
William J. Bain, Sr.
Clifton Brady
Perry B. Johanson

Kalman H. Axelrod
Richard A. Beach
Douglas A. Bevis
William H. Bigelow, III
Robert G. Burke
Deborah L. DeGabrielle
James W. Evans
Donald A. Flynn
Robert L. Gilley
James Godwin
James A. Gresham
David P. Haworth
Albert E. Hennessy
Thomas R. Hickman
Patrick T. James
Richard J. Koopman
James L. Larson
Melvin J. Larson
Herbert K.C. Luke
Richard A. Mangum
Paul Mar
Marian C. Martin
Kenneth D. Maynard
Robert E. Messer
David L. Noferi
Howard A. Partch
Robert J. Pope
Eric C. Rising
Derek J. Selfe
Robert R. Sowder
L. Dixon Steinbright
William Svensson
Michael Trower
David R. Vadman
Gordon K. Walker
Harry G. Widener
Donald A. Winkelmann

Biographies

Neil Anderson, AIA
Partner

Appointed NBBJ's eastern region CEO in 1997, and as principal in charge of health care architecture in the East, Neil Anderson defines his role at NBBJ as hands-on integrator and facilitator. As the former, he shepherds the firm's creativity, expertise, and resources into a unified process centered around client needs.

Anderson joined NBBJ in 1980 after work with Quinlivan Pierik & Krause (Syracuse, New York), Mercury Consultants (Tehran, London, Paris), Carl A. Worthington & Associates (Boulder, Colorado), and Kleb Shelp & Associates (Aurora, Illinois). Anderson earned his Bachelor of Architecture degree in 1970 from Notre Dame University, and his Master of Architecture in 1974 from the University of Colorado. He was made a partner in 1994.

Among his numerous projects covering a wide range of building sizes and types are the Koo Foundation Cancer Center in Taipei, Taiwan; the University of Birjand, Iran, Master Plan; and Genesys Regional Medical Center, Grand Blanc, MI, the first facility designed for patient-focused care.

In a world of specialists, Anderson remains an accomplished generalist, and his breadth of significant health care experience in the United States and abroad gives him the expertise to recognize this demanding area's special needs and concerns. He has lectured on "Design as an Explicit Problem-Solving Process," and in May 1995 he presented "The Impact of Organizational Re-Engineering on the Patient-Focused Care Hospital" (with Dan White) at the International Hospital Federation's 29th International Hospital Congress in Budapest, Hungary.

William J. Bain, Jr., FAIA, MRAIC
Partner

Bill Bain, Jr. joined Naramore Bain Brady & Johanson in 1955 with the imperative to improve the firm's design services and reputation. His success in this endeavor is evident not only from the numerous projects he has designed or supervised, but also from the cultural change in the firm that began with his elevation to partner in 1961. Since that time, NBBJ has found excellence through scrupulous selection of talented architects and support personnel, assiduous attention to detail, and consistent emphasis on superior client services. During his four decades with the company, NBBJ has evolved from a respected regional practice to an acclaimed international competitor recognized with more than 300 awards.

Bain earned his Bachelor degree in Architecture from Cornell University in 1953. While there, he garnered two major design awards: the York Prize (1949) and the Charles Goodwin Sands Memorial Medal (1953). After two years service in Port Whittier, Alaska, as a First Lieutenant with the Army Corps of Engineers, he returned to Seattle and within six years was a partner in Naramore Bain Brady & Johanson.

Described by a former NBBJ principal as "the heart and soul of the firm," Bain is particularly adept at historic rehabilitation and renovation, leading restorations of Seattle's landmark Four Seasons Olympic Hotel and Paramount Theater, and of Sun Mountain Resort in Eastern Washington (which received *Interiors* magazine's "Best in Hotel Design" award in 1991).

Active in the Seattle community for four decades, Bain participates in, and has often led, most of the important commercial, civic, and arts organizations. Among these are the Seattle Downtown Association (Board of Directors since 1980, Chairman 1991–92), the Seattle Chamber of Commerce (Board of Directors 1980–83, 1991–92), the Corporate Council for the Arts (Board of Directors), the Henry Art Gallery Association, the Rotary Club of Seattle (Board of Directors 1970–72), and Enterprise Forum. His 25-year volunteer relationship with the Seattle Symphony Orchestra has included board membership (1974–87) and presidency (1977–79). Bain has also served as president of both the Seattle Chapter and Washington State Council of the American Institute of Architects.

As a visiting critic, juror, and lecturer at the University of Washington, Washington State University, Cornell University, and professional forums, Bain has discussed or published on such topics as "Rehabilitating a Building," "Discontinuities in Educational Facilities Design 1980," "Are Cities Doomed?," "Pacific Rim Perspective: Design in a Global Marketplace," "Design Management for Practicing Architects," "The Design of Non-Traditional Research Laboratory Facilities," "The Future of Residential Architecture," and "Design Process Techniques." He has also acted as juror for the Progressive Architecture Design Awards Program and several AIA Chapter Honor Awards programs. He is listed in *Who's Who in the West, … in America,* and *… in the World.*

Friedrich K.M. Böhm, FAIA, AICP
Partner

NBBJ's Chairman concerns himself with the firm's long-term strategic direction while championing the Renaissance ideal of architect as perceptive and ethical designer, teacher, community leader, and businessman. As city planner, entrepreneur, manager, architect, educator, and diplomat, Friedl Böhm engages life with a zestful mastery of eclectic disciplines. As a practitioner of architectural and urban design, he offers every project a uniquely rich, full-spectrum perspective particularly noteworthy for its integrated and balanced understanding of aesthetic, economic, and community requirements.

Functioning as an advisor or leader on many of NBBJ's Eastern Region projects (based in Columbus, Ohio), Böhm stays especially active in a design and planning capacity on those requiring his expertise in large, complex urban developments. Böhm has been credited with helping define the modern character of downtown Columbus as both community leader and architect, setting the standards for its thoughtful development with such prominent structures as the Wexner Institute for Pediatric Research, Three Nationwide Plaza, the Vern Riffe Center for Government and the Arts, and several downtown high-rise structures.

Born in Krems, Austria, in 1942, Böhm lived in Soviet-occupied territory until 1955. In 1966, he received his Master degree in Architecture (Dipl. Ing.) from the University of Vienna.

A Fulbright Scholar, he received his Master degree in City and Regional Planning in 1969 at Ohio State University (having also completed extensive studies in Business Administration).

Continued

His relationship with the school continues today, with recognition in 1988 as a Distinguished Alumnus, and positions from 1969–73 as a lecturer and since 1986 as an adjunct professor. He also serves on the Board of Directors of the OSU School of Architecture.

In 1968, Böhm joined architects Chuck Nietschke and Jim Godwin as an architect and planner, and within a year had established an eight-member urban planning group at the center of Nietschke-Godwin-Böhm. Just six years later, N-G-B came to the attention of NBBJ as the ideal local firm to oversee the new Ohio Center convention complex. That relationship established the bonds that led to merger in 1977. Böhm became Managing Partner of NBBJ in 1987.

In 1991, Böhm was named Entrepreneur of the Year by *Inc.* magazine and the Institute of American Entrepreneurs. He has served on the Board of Directors of several public companies, including the Huntington National Bank and M.I. Schottenstein Homes.

Böhm also serves the community as current or former board member of the Wellington School (former chairman), Muskingum College, the Columbus Symphony Orchestra, and the Columbus Museum of Art. As a diplomat, Böhm has served on the Special Advisory Committee to the Austrian Chancellor, was named Honorary Consul for Austria in 1993, and in 1995 received the Grand Decoration of Honors in Silver for Services to the Republic of Austria.

Among Böhm's public addresses are "The Architect's Role In Society" (AIA 1996), "High Technology in Campus Buildings" (at the Third International Symposium on Preserving a Quality Environment for Learning, Belgium 1989), and a speech before the International Symposium on Entrepreneurship (Vienna 1990). His published articles include "Birth of a New Town" and "Revitalization of Downtown." He is listed in *Who's Who in America* and ... *in the World,* and in *Outstanding Young Men in America.*

Lawrence E. Helman, AICP
Partner

As NBBJ's partner in charge of planning, Larry Helman is instrumental in resolving complex planning issues by addressing long-term direction with short-term action—particularly for clients with multiple constituencies. His in-depth knowledge of health care, higher education, government, development, and community planning proves uniquely beneficial to clients in achieving successful mixed-use project goals.

Helman joined NBBJ in 1970 shortly after earning his Bachelor of Science degree in Business Administration (Community Analysis major) from Ohio State University. He received his Master of City and Regional Planning degree from Ohio State University in 1972, graduating at the top of his class.

Helman was made a partner in 1988 and has managed diverse planning projects throughout the United States. His experience encompasses master planning, facility programming and locational analysis, development and redevelopment planning, and a wide range of community-based urban planning and corridor studies. Helman's special forté in campus master planning has placed him as project partner on more than 25 major campus master planning projects.

Among his many projects are a 4,000-acre "new town" for the New Albany Company, a breakthrough patient-focused health care project for Genesys Health System, campus and neighborhood redevelopment for the Children's Hospital in Denver, Colorado, and master plans for Ohio State University, Cornell University, and Cleveland State University.

Helman has spoken at the Society for College and University Planners Conference, and the Midwest Facilities Planning Conference. He has also lectured at Ohio State University City and Regional Planning Graduate School and the Columbus Chamber of Commerce. His civic and professional associations include the American Planning Association, the Ohio Planning Conference, the National Trust for Historic Preservation, and the National Association of Office and Industrial Parks.

Helman is registered with the American Institute of Certified Planners (1978).

David C. Hoedemaker, FAIA
Partner

The driving force of NBBJ's design excellence, David Hoedemaker has for three decades led many of the firm's most acclaimed projects, and garnered numerous prestigious design awards. As Managing Partner from 1975 to 1987, he oversaw the beginning of the company's expansion to national and international markets, its strategic association (and often merger) with smaller firms, and its transformation from a respected regional practice to an international competitor.

Hoedemaker came to NBBJ in 1962 after work with Eero Saarinen in Michigan and Connecticut, and with A.O. Baumgardner and Paul Hayden Kirk in Seattle. He piloted jet fighters on active duty with the US Air Force between earning a Bachelor of Arts degree in Architecture from Stanford University (1955) and a Bachelor of Architecture degree from the University of Washington (1960). The AIA awarded Hoedemaker honors at both Stanford (a High Scholarship award, 1955) and the UW (the Henry Adams Fund Award, 1960), and he received a High Scholarship Award from the UW (1960) and the annual Traveling Scholarship from the UW College of Architecture and Urban Planning (1959). He received his Master of Architecture degree from Yale University in 1962. In 1985 he received a mid-career fellowship for study in Rome.

Having joined NBBJ as a designer, Hoedemaker became a partner in 1968, and Managing Partner and CEO in 1976. As such, he led NBBJ through the difficult transition from first-generation to second-generation leadership, and from regional to national practice, with an acumen for strategic planning that both strengthened the firm's design capabilities and created key alliances with smaller firms.

In 1983, Hoedemaker passed CEO responsibilities to Jim Jonassen. In 1987, Friedl Böhm assumed the responsibility of Managing Partner and Hoedemaker became NBBJ's first Partner in Charge of Design.

Among his numerous projects are the new Pacific Northwest Baseball Park, Sea-Tac International Airport Concourse Expansion, Battelle Research Center (Seattle), the Salk Institute's Cancer Research Animal Facility, the National Oceanic & Atmospheric Administration's Western Regional Center, Sitka (Alaska) Native Village Revitalization, the Washington Technology Center (UW Fluke Hall), Pomona Valley (California) Hospital Women's Center, the Seattle Fisheries Center, and Bellevue Community College.

Hoedemaker serves on the National AIA Design Committee, and has served the Seattle AIA Chapter as board member (1970–74) and president (1973). He was elected a Fellow of the AIA in 1979. Other civic associations include the UW Rome Center Advisory Board (1995 to present), the Northwest Institute for Urban Studies in Italy (board 1986–90, president 1987), the Senior Council of Architects (president 1978), the Washington State Council of Architects (board 1972–74), the UW College of Architecture and Urban Planning Visiting Committee, Seattle Central Community College Development Board (1984–86), the Seattle Art Museum (board and executive committee 1976–93), and the Seattle Children's Home (board 1993–96, president 1997).

As an advisor, visiting lecturer, and critic for the UW College of Architecture and Urban Planning, Hoedemaker has lectured there and elsewhere. His presentations include "Freedom and Uncertainty in the Post-Modern Era: In Search of A New Paradigm in Architectural Design," "Learning from Rome: Lessons for Seattle," "Planning and Designing Cities: The Role of the Visionary," "Project Management: An Architect's Perspective," "Mergers and Acquisitions," and "Marketing from a Large Firm Perspective." He has served on numerous national and regional design award juries.

James O. Jonassen, FAIA, MRAIC
Partner

As Managing Partner of NBBJ, Jim focuses his managerial skills on the performance of NBBJ's studios and on the firm's world-wide practice. Fostering a quality of leadership that encourages diversity of thought and superior responsiveness to clients, Jonassen consistently challenges and inspires NBBJ staff to achieve the best possible balance of design, technology, management process, and communication. Many of his projects have won design awards.

Jonassen's active, hands-on involvement in the creative conception and design of his projects is well-known among his clients, which have included many of the most prominent providers in the health care and research fields: Battelle Memorial Institute, the Mayo Clinic, the Veterans Administration, Stanford University Hospital, David Grant Medical Center at Travis AFB (California), the University of California at Davis Medical Center, Assisted Living of America, Swedish Medical Center (Seattle), the University of Washington Medical Center, the University of Rochester Ambulatory Care Center, the Fred Hutchinson Cancer Center (Seattle), and many children's hospitals in Seattle, Spokane, San Diego, Chicago, Shanghai, and elsewhere. He currently pursues an active Asian portfolio with numerous projects in China and Korea.

Jonassen earned his Bachelor of Architecture degree from the University of Washington in 1964, and his Master of Science in Architecture from Columbia University in 1965 on full scholarship. He joined NBBJ immediately upon graduation, and soon became a specialist in medical service and research facilities—though perhaps against expectation.

"I didn't have any interest in the health care field when I started out," he has said. "But after I'd been here a while I won a research grant to study health facilities in Europe, and I became fascinated with the possibilities."

That fascination and his continuous research quickly established Jonassen's national reputation as a health care futurist. Approaching the field with unusual circumspection, he develops each health facility as a total piece of architecture that integrates function, design, place, and healing. His research has led him to design healing environments through assiduous consideration of aesthetic form and color, lighting (especially daylight), air quality, materials, sound, and artwork. As Jonassen notes, "The facility environment can contribute directly to the patient's healing experience."

This concise observation has been proven time and again through NBBJ's detailed research and application, and through response to its many projects, perhaps most dramatically of all the Patient Care Pavilion at the Children's Hospital and Health Center (San Diego), an iconoclastic facility lavishly praised by patients, their parents, and staff.

Described by a former NBBJ principal as the company's "steel rod, focused and disciplined," Jonassen became a full partner in 1970, and CEO of the Western Region in 1983. *Time* magazine named him one of its "Top Young Citizens" in 1978, and *Wide Awake in Seattle,* a book on leadership, featured him as one of 11 exemplary civic and business leaders in the region.

His personal credo—"To be honest with yourself, you have to give more than people expect to receive"—informs his professional and civic associations as much as his work. He serves the AIA as a member of its Large Firm Roundtable, Academy of Architecture for Health, Health Facilities Research & Education Program, Federal Agency Liaison Group, and as past chairman of its National Committee of Architecture for Health and past member of both its National Committee for Architecture for Commerce and Industry (Steering Committee) and its Life Cycle Cost Task Force. Other memberships include the Public Health Group, the International Union of Architects, and the Health Insights think tank, and board memberships with the School Zone Institute, Swedish Medical Center Foundation, and the Seattle Architecture Foundation (past). He was elected to the College of Fellows of the AIA in 1986.

A frequent lecturer, Jonassen has shared his expertise and vision at the universities of Kansas, Meiji (Tokyo), Nagoya (Tokyo), Nebraska, Washington, Clemson (Wisconsin), and Texas A&M. Among his prolific presentations and published articles are several lectures before the International Hospital Federation, "New Directions for Health Facilities: A Value-Driven View" (*Journal of Healthcare Design*, 1995), "Design Strategies to Assist Healing" (*Hospital Management International*, 1995), and "The Future of Healthcare Architecture" (*Healthcare Strategic Management*, 1987).

"Jim Jonassen is a stellar example of getting people to maintain a focus, and maintain a quality of architecture and service to clients while maintaining the business," said Hugh Hochberg, president of management consulting firm The Coxe Group. "NBBJ is the best managed of the large firms."

John R. Pangrazio, AIA
Partner

John Pangrazio has devoted his entire career to health care architecture. But while concerned with resolving contemporary challenges, he remains steadfast in his commitment to planning strategies that anticipate and meet the needs of the future.

Pangrazio hones his substantial expertise in hospital planning and management by meeting regularly with hospital administrators and professionals to discuss problems and identify opportunities for rational, responsive design. He maintains hands-on responsibility throughout the life of each project he undertakes. With more than three dozen health care clients during his 25-year career, his projects have included acute care hospitals, ambulatory care facilities, and medical office buildings.

A Master of Architecture from the University of Washington (1971), Pangrazio first earned his Bachelor of Architecture from California Polytechnic State Institute (1967) and served the Air Force for three years as an architect with the Medical Service Corps. He joined NBBJ in 1974 after work with several small firms, was made an associate in 1975, Director of Health Care Architecture in 1982, and partner in 1987, when he moved to San Francisco to supervise the studio there. Pangrazio's primary focus in recent years has been guiding NBBJ's burgeoning work in Southeast Asia.

Among his numerous projects are the Proton Beam Therapy Unit at California's Loma Linda University Medical Center (with which he has enjoyed a 10-year relationship), the Master Plan for John Muir Medical Center, the Los Angeles Children's Hospital, the University of California at Davis Medical Center, San Joaquin (California) Mental Health Services, Merritt Peralta Medical Center (Oakland, California), the Mayo Clinic (Rochester, New York), Central Washington Hospital, and Harborview Medical Center (Seattle, Washington).

Continued

A member of the Healthcare Forum, the AIA Committee on Architecture for Health (chairman of the Design Subcommittee), and the national Health Insights think tank, Pangrazio also publishes and lectures extensively on the health care industry for both professionals and architectural students, averaging two public speaking engagements a year for the past decade. Among his articles and speeches are "What Makes A Medical Office Building Competitive?" (*Hospitals,* 1982), "Designing the Hospital-Based Medical Office Building" (*Healthcare Financial Management,* 1983), "Planning for Technology" (Association of Western Hospitals Instruction Conference, 1985), "An Evaluation of the Interstitial Space Concept in Health Facility Design" (1970), and "The Impact of National Health Insurance on Facility Planning and Design" (1970).

Pangrazio holds registration as an architect in California and Washington, and with the NCARB (1973). He is a member of the American Association for Hospital Planning, the Architectural Advisory Panel of the Association for the Care of Children's Health, the Medical Group Management Association (corresponding member, 1980–90), and the Group Health Association of America.

Scott Wyatt, FAIA
Partner

Appointed western regional CEO of NBBJ in 1997, Scott is responsible for the performance of the western offices of the firm. Recognized throughout his career for sophisticated and functional corporate design, Scott Wyatt wed his highly successful Wyatt Architects (formerly Wyatt Stapper Architects) to NBBJ in 1991 after more than a decade of success with major corporate clients.

Wyatt has a special ability to translate a company's vision, purpose, and culture into elegant facilities that integrate interiors with building structure, character, and landscape. For more than 20 years, his practice has focused on helping corporations create environments that enhance and inspire creativity and productivity with comfort, accessibility, and meaning. His touchstones in designing a given space are client identity and character of leadership, services and products, and reputation and position within the market.

Among Wyatt's many clients are Immunex, Burger King, Nike, Merrill Lynch, Westin Hotel, Adobe, IBM, Maersk, KPMG-Peat Marwick, Lotus, Elgin Syferd (Needham), Microsoft, Teledesic, Cole & Webber (Ogilvey), and ZymoGenetics. His work has been recognized with numerous design awards (including a national Institute of Business Design Silver Award in 1985), and with feature publications in such magazines as *Architecture, Interiors, Progressive Architecture, Architectural Record, Interior Design, Northwest Design & Living, Designers West,* and *Washington CEO.* In 1990, Wyatt sat with nine other architects on the AIA Design Excellence Roundtable on Interiors in Washington, DC.

After earning dual Bachelor degrees (in Architecture and Building Science) from Rensselaer Polytechnical Institute in 1972, Wyatt spent two years with the Peace Corps working for the Tehran (Iran) Planning Office before joining Seattle's Lovegren Loveland & Associates in 1975. Within five years, that company had evolved from Loveland Stapper Wyatt into Wyatt Stapper Architects, a group of 70 designers that became known simply as Wyatt Architects by 1990.

In 1991, he joined his firm with NBBJ as a principal leading a combined studio of specialists in interior and corporate design. As partner since 1994, his responsibilities include management and leadership of NBBJ Corporate Design, with projects executed through six offices nationwide.

Wyatt serves the boards of directors of the Seattle Architectural Foundation, the Seattle Opera (Vice President, 1990), KUOW Public Radio, ArtFair Seattle (founding member), the Henry Art Gallery (1995), and the Seattle Children's Home (1989–91). His memberships include the Seattle Architects Roundtable, Rotary Club, Corporate Council for the Arts, the Urban Land Institute (1988–90), the National Trust for Historic Preservation (1984–88), and United Way (associate chair and chair, 1985–86).

Wyatt became a Fellow of the American Institute of Architects in 1993.

David R. Zimmerman, CPA
Partner

David Zimmerman holds primary responsibility for business and financial management of all eastern operations. Working through NBBJ's Columbus office, Zimmerman also participates in contract negotiations, automation systems, personnel management, project budgeting and control, and business planning for the NBBJ Profit Sharing Trust. As a member of the firm's Partnership Executive Committee, he oversees general business matters and financial and risk management for NBBJ.

Zimmerman earned his Bachelor of Science degree in Accounting from Florida State University in 1968. After a tour as Second Lieutenant in the United States Army (1969–71) and three years with the First Columbus Corporation (1971–74), Zimmerman joined NBBJ in 1974 and subsequently completed his Master of Business Administration degree at Capital University in 1982. He was made a partner in 1987.

A Certified Public Accountant registered in Ohio since 1975, he serves with the Ohio Society of CPAs and the Professional Services Management Association. His lectures at the Ohio State University Graduate School include "Architectural Firm Affiliations: Temporary and Permanent."

Active in civic affairs, Zimmerman has sat on the advisory board of the National Kidney Foundation of Ohio, and the board of trustees of the Columbus Swim & Racquet Club (past president). For Upper Arlington High School, he has contributed to the Board of Education Special Task Force to Evaluate Programs.

Selected Chronological List
of Buildings & Projects

Renaissance Infill Housing
Columbus, Ohio
1981
Client: Olentangy Management Company

Westmoreland County Complex
Greensburg, Pennsylvania
July 1983
Client: Westmoreland County

**National Oceanic Administration Association,
Western Regional Center**
Seattle, Washington
January 1984
Client: US Department of Commerce

Wyoming Women's Center
Cheyenne, Wyoming
July 1984
Client: Wyoming Women's Center

**Headquarters Building,
Episcopal Diocese of East Carolina**
Kinston, North Carolina
1985
Client: Episcopal Diocese of East Carolina

Old, Old Post Office
Columbus, Ohio
January 1986
Client: Bricker & Eckler Building Company

Key Bank Tower
Seattle, Washington
January 1987
Client: Martin Selig Real Estate

The Biomembrane Institute,
Research & Development Laboratory
Seattle, Washington
May 1987
Client: The Biomembrane Institute

Vern Riffe Center
for Government and the Arts
Columbus, Ohio
January 1988
Client: Ohio Building Authority

USAF, David Grant Medical Center
Fairfield, California
October 1988
Client: United States Air Force

Atrium at Three Nationwide Plaza
Columbus, Ohio
June 1989
Client: Nationwide Insurance

University of Arizona
College of Architecture Remodel
Tucson, Arizona
August 1989
Client: University of Arizona,
College of Architecture

Thoits Building
Palo Alto, California
January 1990
Client: Thoits Brothers Inc.

Davis Wright & Jones
Seattle, Washington
June 1990
Client: Davis Wright & Jones

Valley Radiation Oncology Center
Los Angeles, California
February 1991
Client: Saint Joseph Medical Center

**Loma Linda University Medical Center,
South Wing Phase II, Proton Beam Therapy**
Loma Linda, California
March 1991
Client: Loma Linda University Medical
Center

Univar
Kirkland, Washington
September 1991
Client: Univar Corporation

Gump's
San Francisco, California
November 1991
Client: Gump's

Children's Fountain
Columbus, Ohio
April 1992
Client: City of Columbus,
Recreation & Parks Department

Franklin Park Conservatory
Columbus, Ohio
April 1992
Joint Recreational District: City of Columbus,
Client: Franklin County and State of Ohio

**University Medical Center,
East Parking Garage**
Tucson, Arizona
June 1992
Client: University Medical Center

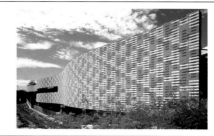

Rosalie Whyel Museum of Doll Art
Bellevue, Washington
September 1992
Client: Doll Art, Inc.

Rose Elementary School
Tucson, Arizona
January 1993
Client: Tucson Unified School District

**Saint Joseph Medical Center,
Robertson Tower**
Burbank, California
April 1993
Client: Saint Joseph Medical Center

**National Taiwan University
Childrens Hospital**
Taiei, Taiwan,R.C.O.
January 1997
Client: National Taiwan University
Childrens Hospital

United Artists, Cinecitta Competition
Rome, Italy
November 1996
Client: U.A. Theater Circuit, Inc.
Eaglewood, Colorado

**El Presidente, Apartment/
Office Tower (45 stories)**
Manila, Philippines
February 1997
Client: Duvay Corporation

Selected Design Awards

Projects Won by Design Competition

Pacific War Memorial, Island of Corregidor, The Philippines

Academy for Contemporary Problems, Columbus, Ohio

Honolulu Municipal Office Building, Honolulu, Hawaii

Glaxo Wellcome Visitors Center, North Carolina

Cosco Headquarters (Chinese Overseas Shipping Company), Beijing, People's Republic of China

Ma-Tsao Resort, Taiwan

Kangbok Hospital, South Korea

Masan Hospital, South Korea

Global Gateway, South Korea

Miller Park (Milwaukee Brewers Retractable Roof Ballpark)

Dayton Cultural and Commercial Center

Taipei Children's Hospital

Aultman Hospital Medical Office Building and Campus Expansion, Ohio

Framingham Senior Housing, Massachusetts

Microsoft Executive Briefing Center, Washington

Genesys Health System, Michigan

Architectural Awards

Merit Award
American Institute of Architects, Ohio Chapter
Howard E. LeFevre Hall, Central Ohio Technical College/Ohio State University at Newark
Newark, Ohio
1996

Grand Conceptor Award
American Consulting Engineers Council
KeyArena
Seattle, Washington
1996

Grand Award
Consulting Engineers Council of Washington
KeyArena
Seattle, Washington
1996

Honor Award
American Society of Landscape Architects, Ohio Chapter
The James A. Young Memorial Walk (The JAYwalk)
Ohio Wesleyan University
Delaware, Ohio
1996

Honor Award
American Institute of Architects, Ohio Chapter
Aultman Hospital Addition/ Renovation
Canton, Ohio
1995

Merit Award
American Institute of Architects, North Carolina Chapter
Cary Chamber of Commerce
Cary, North Carolina
1995

Honor Award
American Institute of Architects, Ohio Chapter
McAlister Studio 30-Minute Photo
Columbus, Ohio
1995

Isosceles Award
American Institute of Architects, Raleigh/Durham/ Chapel Hill Section
Moore Regional Health and Fitness Center
Pinehurst, North Carolina
1995

Excellence in Design Award
Design & Build New York (published jointly by the General Contractors/NYS and American Institute of Architects New York State)
Weinberg Campus (Menorah Campus)
Amherst, New York
1995

Office Development of the Year
Society of Industrial Office Realtors, Washington Chapter
West Lake Union Center
Seattle, Washington
1995

Honor Award
American Institute of Architects, Northwest and Pacific Region
ZymoGenetics Steam Plant
Seattle, Washington
1995

Honor Award
American Institute of Architects, Seattle Chapter
ZymoGenetics Steam Plant
Seattle, Washington
1995

Honor Award
American Institute of Architects, Columbus Chapter
Clark State Community College,
Performing Arts Center
Springfield, Ohio
1994

Project of the Month
Daily Journal of Commerce/ American Institute of Architects
Everett Community Theater
Everett, Washington
1994

National Honor Award for Interiors
American Institute of Architects
Seafirst Gallery, Columbia Seafirst Center
Seattle, Washington
1994

Design Excellence Award
Department of the Navy
United States Navy Family Support Complex (Smokey Point) Naval Station
Marysville, Washington
1994

Peter F. Drucker Award for Nonprofit Innovation
Weinberg Campus (Menorah Campus)
Amherst, New York
1994

Design for Aging Award
American Institute of Architects/AAHSA
Weinberg Campus (Menorah Campus)
Amherst, New York
1994

American Institute of Architects Health Facilities Review
Central Washington Hospital Additions
Wenatchee, Washington
1993

Special Recognition
American Society of Landscape Architects, Ohio Chapter
Children's Fountain
Columbus, Ohio
1993

Design Health Care Award
Modern Healthcare
Children's Hospital and Health Center, Patient Care Pavilion
San Diego, California
1993

Honor Award
American Institute of Architects, Columbus Chapter
Columbus State Community College, Harold M. Nester Academic Center
Columbus, Ohio
1993

Honor Award
The Institute of Business Designers/Columbus Interior Design Awards
Columbus State Community College, Harold M. Nester Academic Center
Columbus, Ohio
1993

Finalist, James B. Recchie Design Awards
Columbus State Community College, Harold M. Nester Academic Center
Columbus, Ohio
1993

Mayor's Award of Excellence for Community Development
Hemlock Bluff
Cary, North Carolina
1993

Honor Award
American Institute of Architects, Columbus Chapter
Howard E. LeFevre Hall
Central Ohio Technical College/Ohio State University at Newark
Newark, Ohio
1993

Merit Award
American Society of Landscape
Architects, Ohio Chapter
Kenyon College Campus
Master Plan
Gambier, Ohio
1993

**American Institute of
Architects Health Facilities
Review**
Pomona Valley Hospital
Medical Women's Center
Pomona, California
1993

Special Recognition
American Society of Landscape
Architects, Ohio Chapter
Rehabilitation Hospital of
Indiana
Indianapolis, Indiana
1993

Honor Award
American Institute of
Architects, Seattle Chapter
Seafirst Gallery, Columbia
Seafirst Center
Seattle, Washington
1993

Building of the Year
Building Owners and Managers
Association, Seattle/King
County Chapter
Two Union Square
Seattle, Washington
1993

Honor Award
American Institute of
Architects, Columbus Chapter
Washington State Community
College
Marietta, Ohio
1993

Design for Aging Award
American Institute of
Architects
Weinberg Campus (Menorah
Campus)
Amherst, New York
1993

AIA Merit Award
Architects Society of Ohio
Worthington Kilbourne High
School
Worthington, Ohio
1993

Honor Award
American Institute of
Architects, Northwest Region
Fluke Hall
University of Washington
Seattle, Washington
1992

Honor Award
American Institute of
Architects, Columbus Chapter
Franklin Park Conservatory
Expansion
Columbus, Ohio
1992

**Office Building of the Year,
International Award Winner,
Government Building Category**
Building Owners and Managers
Association
National Oceanic and
Atmospheric Administration
(NOAA), Western Regional
Center
Seattle, Washington
1992

**Office Building of the Year,
Regional Award Winner,
Historical Buildings Category**
Building Owners and Managers
Association
Old, Old Post Office
Columbus, Ohio
1992

Mayor's Award of Excellence
Resurrection Lutheran Church
Cary, North Carolina
1992

**Office Building of the Year,
Regional Award Winner,
Corporate Headquarters
Category**
Building Owners and Managers
Association
Security Pacific Tower
Seattle, Washington
1992

**Gold Key Award Finalist
(Guestrooms and Suites)**
Hospitality Design magazine
Sun Mountain Resort
Winthrop, Washington
1992

**Office Building of the Year,
Regional Award Winner**
Building Owners and Managers
Association
Three Nationwide Plaza
Columbus, Ohio
1992

**Honor Award for Excellence in
Architecture**
American Institute of
Architects, Western Mountain
Region
Tucson Arizona State Office
Building
Tucson, Arizona
1992

Citation Award
American Institute of
Architects, Southern Arizona
Chapter
Tucson Arizona State Office
Building
Tucson, Arizona
1992

Citation Award
American Institute of
Architects, Southern Arizona
Chapter
University of Arizona Medical
Center, East Parking Structure
Tucson, Arizona
1992

Design for Aging Award
American Institute of
Architects/AAHSA
Weinberg Campus (Menorah
Campus)
Amherst, New York
1992

Honor Award
American Institute of
Architects, Columbus Chapter
Worthington Kilbourne High
School
Worthington, Ohio
1992

Excellence in Design Award
Secretary of Defense
David Grant Medical Center
Travis Air Force Base
Fairfield, California
1991

Honor Award
American Institute of
Architects, Western Mountain
Region
DeMiguel Elementary School
Flagstaff, Arizona
1991

Honor Award
American Institute of
Architects, Seattle Chapter
Fluke Hall
University of Washington
Seattle, Washington
1991

**Best in Executive Office
Design**
Interiors magazine
Great Northern Insured
Annuity
Seattle, Washington
1991

Honor Award
American Institute of
Architects, Seattle Chapter
Herring Newman Direct
Response Advertising
Seattle, Washington
1991

Merit Award
American Institute of
Architects, Northwest Region
Market Place Tower
Seattle, Washington
1991

Merit Award
American Institute of
Architects, Seattle Chapter
Providence Medical Center,
East Wing Addition
Seattle, Washington
1991

**Merit Award,
Isosceles Awards Program**
American Institute of
Architects, Raleigh and
Durham/Chapel Hill Chapter
Resurrection Lutheran Church
Cary, North Carolina
1991

**Outstanding Achievement
Award**
The Institute of Business
Designers and Interior Design
magazine
Squire Sanders & Dempsey
Columbus, Ohio
1991

Merit Award
Columbus Interior Design
Awards
The Institute of Business
Designers
Squire Sanders & Dempsey
Columbus, Ohio
1991

Best in Hotel Design Award
Interiors magazine
Sun Mountain Resort
Winthrop, Washington
1991

**Design Award,
New Construction Category**
City of Palo Alto Architecture
Review Board
Thoits Building
Palo Alto, California
1991

Honor Award
American Institute of
Architects, Northwest Region
Two Union Square
Seattle, Washington
1991

Honor Award
American Institute of
Architects, Columbus Chapter
Vern Riffe Center for
Government and the Arts
Columbus, Ohio
1991

Honor Award
American Institute of
Architects, Columbus Chapter
Bank One Financial
Marketplace
Dublin, Ohio
1990

City Beautiful Award
Columbus Convention and
Visitors Bureau
The Brewery District
Columbus, Ohio
1990

Honorable Mention
Specialty Department Store
Design Competition
Institute of Store Planners and
Visual Merchandising and
Store Design
Brooks Brothers, Tower City
Cleveland, Ohio
1990

Merit Award
Isosceles Awards Program
American Institute of
Architects, Raleigh and
Durham/Chapel Hill Sections
Burroughs Wellcome
Company, Corporate Visitors
Center
Research Triangle Park, North
Carolina
1990

Merit Award
American Institute of
Architects, Southern Arizona
Chapter
Canyon View Elementary
School
Tucson, Arizona
1990

Award of Excellence
American Institute of
Architects/National Concrete
Masonry Association
Chet Paulson Outfitters
Tacoma, Washington
1990

**City of Los Angeles Award of
Design Excellence**
The Los Angeles Board of
Cultural Affairs
Children's Hospital De
Longpre Avenue Pedestrian
Bridge
Los Angeles, California
1990

Merit Award
American Institute of
Architects, North Carolina
Chapter
Christian Science Reading
Room
Raleigh, North Carolina
1990

Honor Award
Sir Walter Raleigh Award for
Community Appearance
City of Raleigh
Christian Science Reading
Room
Raleigh, North Carolina
1990

Honor Award
American Institute of
Architects, Southern Arizona
Chapter
De Miguel Elementary School
Flagstaff, Arizona
1990

Honor Award
Institute of Business Designers
Market Place Tower
Seattle, Washington
1990

Merit Award
American Institute of
Architects, Seattle Chapter
Market Place Tower
Seattle, Washington
1990

Award of Excellence
Institute of Business Designers
Moss Adams
Seattle, Washington
1990

**Merit Award, Unbuilt
Commissioned Projects**
Isosceles Awards Program
American Institute of
Architects, Raleigh and Chapel
Hill/ Durham Section
North Carolina Indian Cultural
Center, Visitor Center
Pembroke, North Carolina
1990

**American Institute of
Architects Health Facilities
Review**
Ohio State University, Arthur
G. James Cancer Hospital and
Research Institute
Columbus, Ohio
1990

City Beautiful Award
Columbus Convention and
Visitors Bureau
Ohio State University, Arthur
G. James Cancer Hospital and
Research Institute
Columbus, Ohio
1990

James B. Reechie Design Award
Old, Old Post Office
Columbus, Ohio
1990

Merit Award
American Institute of
Architects, North Carolina
Chapter
St Andrew Catholic Church
Apex, North Carolina
1990

Grand Award for Buildings
American Consulting
Engineers Council
Two Union Square
Seattle, Washington
1990

Merit Award
American Institute of
Architects, Seattle Chapter
Two Union Square
Seattle, Washington
1990

Award of Excellence
Best Commercial Project over
150,000 square feet
NAHB/NCBC
Two Union Square
Seattle, Washington
1990

**American Institute of
Architects Health Facilities
Review**
University of Cincinnati
Medical Center, The Charles
M. Barrett Center
Cincinnati, Ohio
1990

Honorary Mention
Institute of Store Planners/
National Retail Merchants
Association
Boyd's Coffee Store
Seattle, Washington
1989

Honor Award
The Institute of Business
Designers
Capitol Theater (in the Vern
Riffe Center for Government
and the Arts)
Columbus, Ohio
1989

**Peggy Ezekiel Award for
Outstanding Achievement in
Theatre Arts**
Capitol Theater (in the Vern
Riffe Center for Government
and the Arts)
Columbus, Ohio
1989

Type I Honor Award
US Air Force
David Grant Medical Center
Travis Air Force Base
Fairfield, California
1989

Award of Excellence
Pacific Northwest Institute
of Business Designers
Hornall Anderson Design
Works
Seattle, Washington
1989

Best of Competition
Pacific Northwest Institute
of Business Designers
Immunex Corporation
Seattle, Washington
1989

Honor Award
The Institute of Business
Designers
McDonald's Restaurant
Columbus, Ohio
1989

Merit Award
American Institute of
Architects, Northwest and
Pacific Region
Merrill Place
Seattle, Washington
1989

Merit Award
American Institute of
Architects, Seattle Chapter
Moss Adams
Seattle, Washington
1989

Honor Award
American Planning Association
and Planning Association of
Washington, Washington
Chapter
Regional Rivershore
Enhancement Plan
Tri-Cities, Washington
1989

Award for Excellence
American Institute of
Architects, North Carolina
Chapter
Sanderling Inn
Sanderling, North Carolina
1989

**People's Choice Award, Best
Commercial Building**
American Institute of
Architects, Seattle Chapter
Two Union Square
Seattle, Washington
1989

**Citation, Triangle Architecture
Awards Program**
Spectator magazine
United States Post Office
Apex, North Carolina
1989

Design Award
Institute of Business Designers
(IBD) and Interior Design
magazine
Cable Langenbach Henry
Edmunds and Kinerk
Seattle, Washington
1988

Citation Award
American Institute of
Architects, Seattle Chapter
Cable Langenbach Henry
Edmunds and Kinerk
Seattle, Washington
1988

**The Walter Taylor Award for
State of the Art Architectural
Design**
American Association of
School Administrators and
American Institute of
Architects Design Awards for
School Architecture
Canyon View Elementary
School
Tucson, Arizona
1988

**Award for Excellence in
Architecture**
American Institute of
Architects, Arizona Society
(State Chapter)
Canyon View Elementary
School
Tucson, Arizona
1988

Special Citation
Secretary of Defense
David Grant Medical Center
Travis Air Force Base
Fairfield, California
1988

Honor Award
American Institute of
Architects, South Atlantic
Region
Episcopal Diocese of East
Carolina Headquarter Building
Kinston, North Carolina
1988

Honor Award
Interfaith Forum on Religion,
Art and Architecture
(American Institute of
Architects affiliate)
Episcopal Diocese of East
Carolina Headquarter Building
Kinston, North Carolina
1988

People's Choice Award
American Institute of
Architects, Seattle Chapter
4225 Roosevelt Building
Seattle, Washington
1988

Merit Award
Architectural Design Awards
Program
Interfaith Forum on Religion,
Art, and Architecture
International/Islamic Studies
Center
Shaw University
Raleigh, North Carolina
1988

Office Building of the Year
Building Owners and Managers
Association
1001 Fourth Avenue Plaza
Building
Seattle, Washington
1988

Honorable Mention
Centers and Stores of
Excellence Design Award
Pasta & Co.
Seattle, Washington
1988

**Honorable Mention,
New Stores Division**
Monitor magazine
Pasta & Co.
Seattle, Washington
1988

**American Institute of
Architects Health Facilities
Review**
Providence Downtown
Seattle, Washington
1988

First Place
Centers and Stores of
Excellence Design Award
Red Balloon Company
Seattle, Washington
1988

**Honorable Mention,
New Stores Division**
Monitor magazine
Red Balloon Company
Seattle, Washington
1988

Merit Award
Interfaith Forum on Religion,
Art and Architecture
St Andrew Catholic Church
Apex, North Carolina
1988

Shirley Cooper Award
American Association of
School Administrators and the
American Institute of
Architects
St Gregory's High School,
Multi-Purpose Building
Tucson, Arizona
1988

**Office Building of the Year,
Historic Category**
Building Owners and Managers
Association of Seattle
Tower Building
Seattle, Washington
1988

**Office Building of the Year,
Historic Category**
Building Owners and Managers
Association Western Region
Tower Building
Seattle, Washington
1988

Merit Award
American Planning Association
and Planning Association of
Washington, Washington
Chapter
Bellingham Central Waterfront
Development Plan
Bellingham, Washington
1987

Merit Award
The Institute of Business
Designers
Children First Day Care
Columbus, Ohio
1987

**Site Planning and Design
Award**
American Society of Landscape
Architects, Ohio Chapter
Dennison Park Place
Residential Cluster
Columbus, Ohio
1987

**Residential Triangle
Development Award**
Triangle J Council of
Governments
Dunbarton Pointe
Condominiums
Raleigh, North Carolina
1987

Honor Award
Triangle Architecture Awards
Program
Spectator magazine
International/Islamic Studies
Center
Shaw University
Raleigh, North Carolina
1987

**Winner, Modern Healthcare's
Design Awards Program**
Kimberly Woods
Mental Retardation Housing
Facility
Columbus, Ohio
1987

Design Citation
American Association of
School Administrators
Mountain View High School
Marana School District
Marana, Arizona
(joint Venture with Finical and
Dombrowski)
1987

Building of the Year Award
Building Owners and Managers
Association, Columbus Chapter
Old, Old Post Office
Columbus, Ohio
1987

**Honor Award, Children's
Choice**
American Institute of
Architects, Seattle Chapter
Pasta & Co.
Seattle, Washington
1987

**International Store of the Year
Award**
National Retail Merchants
Association and Institute of
Store Planners (NRMA/ISP)
Red Balloon Company
Seattle, Washington
1987

Merit Award
The Institute of Business
Designers
Schottenstein, Zox & Dunn
Columbus, Ohio
1987

Institutional Award
Triangle Development Award
Program
Triangle J Council of
Governments
Watauga Hall
North Carolina State University
Raleigh, North Carolina
1987

Design Excellence
Eastern Region Department of
the Air Force
ADAL Aircraft Systems
Engineering Facility
Wright-Patterson Air Force
Base, Ohio
1986

Honor Award
American Institute of
Architects, Seattle Chapter
Bagley Wright Theater at
Seattle Center
Seattle, Washington
1986

**American Institute of
Architects Health Facilities
Review**
David Grant Medical Center
Travis Air Force Base
Fairfield, California
1986

**American Institute of
Architects/ACA Exhibition of
Architecture
for Justice**
Eastern Regional Juvenile
Detention Center
Martinsburg, West Virginia
1986

Building of the Year Award
Building Owners and Managers
Association, Columbus Chapter
55 Nationwide Boulevard
Columbus, Ohio
1986

Merit Award
American Society of Landscape
Architects, Washington
Chapter
Hewlett-Packard
Lake Stevens Instrument
Division
Lake Stevens, Washington
1986

City Beautiful Award
Huntington National Bank
Park
Columbus, Ohio
1986

Honor Award
American Institute of
Architects, Architects Society of
Ohio
Huntington Plaza
Columbus, Ohio
1986

Merit Award
American Institute of
Architects, Seattle Chapter
McCann Erickson
Seattle, Washington
1986

Design Award
Combined Student Juries,
University of Arizona and
Arizona State University
Awards Program
Mountain View High School
Marana School District
Marana, Arizona
(joint venture with Finical and
Dombrowski)
1986

**Winner, Modern Healthcare's
Design Awards Program**
Scottsdale Memorial Hospital
North
Scottsdale, Arizona
1986

**American Institute of
Architects Health Facilities
Review**
Scottsdale Memorial Hospital
North
Scottsdale, Arizona
1986

Honor Award
American Institute of
Architects
United States Coast Guard
Administrative Building
Kodiak, Alaska
1986

**Silver Award for Outstanding
Achievement**
National Institute of Business
Designers/Interior Design
magazine
Bannerworks
Seattle, Washington
1985

Renovation of the Year
Tacoma/Pierce County
Building Owners and Managers
Association
Broadway Terrace
Tacoma, Washington
1985

City Beautiful Award
Columbus Convention and
Visitors Bureau
Corporate Exchange Office
Park
Columbus, Ohio
1985

Honor Award
American Institute of
Architects, Columbus Chapter
55 Nationwide Boulevard
Columbus, Ohio
1985

Merit Award
The Institute of Business
Designers
55 Nationwide Boulevard
Columbus, Ohio
1985

Merit Award
The Institute of Business
Designers
Huntington Center, Executive
Floor Offices
Columbus, Ohio
1985

Award for Excellence
American Institute of
Architects, North Carolina
Chapter
International/Islamic Studies
Center
Shaw University
Raleigh, North Carolina
1985

Merit Award
The Institute of Business
Designers
John W. Kessler Offices
Columbus, Ohio
1985

Excellence in Design Award
American Institute of
Architects, Arizona Society
(State Chapter)
Manning Residence
Tucson, Arizona
1985

Honor Award
American Institute of
Architects, Columbus Chapter
Mercy Hospital Anderson
Cincinnati, Ohio
1985

Honor Award
American Institute of
Architects, Seattle Chapter
Merrill Place
Seattle, Washington
1985

Honor Award
American Institute of
Architects, Columbus Chapter
Mid-Ohio Regional Planning
Commission Headquarters
Building
Columbus, Ohio
1985

Merit Award
American Institute of
Architects, South Arizona
Chapter
Mountain View High School
Marana School District
Marana, Arizona
1985

Honor Award
American Institute of
Architects, Columbus Chapter
Our Lady Of Mercy Hospital
Cincinnati, Ohio
1985

Merit Award
The Institute of Business
Designers
The Palace Theater
Columbus, Ohio
1985

**First Place, International Store
Design Competition**
Institute of Store Planners/
National Retail Merchants
Association
Storehouse
Atlanta, Georgia
1985

Merit Award
American Institute of
Architects, Southern Arizona
Chapter
Tortolita Junior High School
Marana School District
Marana, Arizona
(joint venture with Finical and
Dombrowski)
1985

Award of Design Excellence
American Institute of
Architects, Arizona Society
(State Chapter)
Tortolita Junior High School
Marana School District
Marana, Arizona
(joint venture with Finical and
Dombrowski)
1985

Honor Award
American Institute of
Architects, Southern Arizona
Chapter
Western Savings and Loan
Ina and La Cholla
Tucson, Arizona
1985

Home of the Year
Seattle Times/American
Institute of Architects
The Willard Residence
Issaquah, Washington
1985

City Beautiful Award
Columbus Convention and
Visitors Bureau
Leo Yassenoff Jewish Center
Columbus, Ohio
1985

City Beautiful Award
Columbus Convention and
Visitors Bureau
Columbia Gas Corporate
Headquarters
Columbus, Ohio
1984

USAF Honor Award
Concept Design Excellence
David Grant Medical Center
Travis Air Force Base
Fairfield, California
1984

**American Institute of
Architects Honor Award**
Architect's Society of Ohio
55 Nationwide Boulevard
Columbus, Ohio
1984

AAA Five Diamond Award
The Four Seasons Olympic
Hotel
Seattle, Washington
1984

Mobile Four Star Award
The Four Seasons Olympic
Hotel
Seattle, Washington
1984

**American Institute of
Architects/ACA Honor Award**
Architecture for Justice
Exhibition
Lewis & Clark County Criminal
Justice Facility
Helena, Montana
1984

Special Achievement Award
State of Arizona Historic
Preservation
Manning Residence
Tucson, Arizona
1984

Honorable Mention Award
American Planning
Association, Washington
Chapter
Seattle Central Community
College Master Plan
Seattle, Washington
1984

Merit Award
American Planning
Association, Washington
Chapter
Squalicum Harbor Land Use
Plan
Bellingham, Washington
1984

Home of the Month
American Institute of
Architects Northwest Region
The Willard Residence
Issaquah, Washington
1984

**High Honors, Laboratory of
the Year Program**
Industrial Research and
Development magazine
Battelle Memorial Institute,
Marine Research Laboratory
Sequim, Washington
1983

City Beautiful Award
Columbus Convention &
Visitors Bureau
Battelle Riverfront Park
Columbus, Ohio
1983

Mobile Four Star Award
The Four Seasons Olympic
Hotel
Seattle, Washington
1983

**Designers Circle Awards
Competition**
First Place, Lobby Division
First Place, Guestroom Division
First Place, Large Meeting
Room/Ballroom Division
Third Place, Restaurant
Division
Lodging Hospitality magazine
The Four Seasons Olympic
Hotel
Seattle, Washington
1983

Honor Award
American Institute of
Architects, Seattle Chapter
Heritage Building (NBBJ
Headquarters)
Seattle, Washington
1983

**American Institute of
Architects/ACA Honor Award**
Architecture for Justice
Exhibition
Lewis County Jail
Chehalis, Washington
1983

**Citation, Architecture in
Progress**
Kamphoefner Awards Program
Sanderling Inn
Sanderling, North Carolina
1983

City Beautiful Award
Columbus Convention and
Visitors Bureau
Sohio Bethel Road
Columbus, Ohio
1983

**Historic Preservation
Commendation**
Best Rehabilitation/Adaptive
Use Project
Commonwealth of
Pennsylvania Historical and
Museum Commission
Westmoreland County
Courthouse
Greensburg, Pennsylvania
1983

**American Institute of
Architects Honor Award**
Architects Society of Ohio
Westmoreland County
Courthouse
Greensburg, Pennsylvania
1983

County Achievement Award
National Association of
Counties
Westmoreland County
Courthouse
Greensburg, Pennsylvania
1983

Merit Award
National Society of the Friends
of Terra Cotta
Westmoreland County
Courthouse
Greensburg, Pennsylvania
1983

**American Institute of
Architects/ACA Honor Award**
Architecture for Justice
Exhibition
Wyoming Women's Center
Lusk, Wyoming
1983

**Outstanding Planning
Achievement**
Planning Association of
Washington
Bellevue Energy Study
Bellevue, Washington
1982

**American Institute of
Architects Honor Award**
Architects Society of Ohio
Dennison Park Place
Residential Cluster
Columbus, Ohio
1982

City Beautiful Award
Columbus Convention and
Visitors Bureau
Dennison Park Place
Residential Cluster
Columbus, Ohio
1982

Mobile Four Star Award
The Four Seasons Olympic
Hotel
Seattle, Washington
1982

Outstanding Project Award
Washington Trust for Historic
Preservation
The Four Seasons Olympic
Hotel
Seattle, Washington
1982

**American Institute of
Architects/ACA Citation for
Excellence**
King County Correctional
Facility
Seattle, Washington
1982

**American Institute of
Architects Honor Award**
Korea Exchange Bank
Seattle, Washington
1982

**American Institute of
Architects Honor Award**
Architects Society of Ohio
Mid-Ohio Regional Planning
Commission Headquarters
Building
Columbus, Ohio
1982

City Beautiful Award
Columbus Convention and
Visitors Bureau
Ohio Center/Hyatt Regency
Convention Complex
Columbus, Ohio
1982

City Beautiful Award
Columbus Convention and
Visitors Bureau
One Capitol South Office
Building
Columbus, Ohio
1982

**Washington State Highway
Beautification Award**
Ruston Way Human Scale
Design Study
Tacoma, Washington
1982

**American Institute of
Architects/ACA Honor Award**
Architecture for Justice
Exhibition
Skagit County Jail/Public
Safety Building
Mount Vernon, Washington
1982

Honor Award
American Institute of
Architects, Arizona Society
(State Chapter)
Steinfeld Mansion Renovation
Tucson, Arizona
1982

Institutional Design of the Year
Interiors magazine
Washington State Court of
Appeals
Seattle, Washington
1982

Honor Award
American Institute of
Architects, Seattle Chapter
Washington State Court of
Appeals
Seattle, Washington
1982

First Award
American Planning
Association, Washington
Chapter
Downtown Housing Needs
Study
Seattle, Washington
1981

**National Endowment for the
Arts for "Design Achievement"**
Maintenance and Operations
Buildings
Municipality of Metropolitan
Seattle, Washington
1981

Special Award
American Institute of
Architects, Columbus Chapter
Renaissance Infill Housing
Olentangy Management
Company
Columbus, Ohio
1981

Merit Award
American Planning
Association, Washington
Chapter
Vancouver Central Park Design
Guidelines
Vancouver, Washington
1981

**American Institute of
Architects Merit Award**
Arizona Society (State
Chapter)
Western Savings and Loan
Camino Seco and Broadway
Tucson, Arizona
1981

Honor Award
American Institute of
Architects, Baltimore Chapter
Baltimore Convention Center
Baltimore, Maryland
(joint venture with Cochran
Stephenson & Donkervoet,
Baltimore)
1980

Honor Award
American Society of Landscape
Architects, North Carolina
Chapter
Cape Hatteras National
Seashore, Design Manual,
National Park Service, US
Department of the Interior
Cape Hatteras National
Seashore, North Carolina
1980

Merit Award
American Institute of
Architects, Arizona Society
(State Chapter)
Greenlee County Correctional
Facility
Clifton, Greenlee County,
Arizona
1980

Honorable Mention Award
Annual Awards Program
American Planning
Association, Washington
Chapter
Pier 66 Master Plan, Port of
Seattle
Seattle, Washington
1980

Planning Achievement Award
Planning Association of
Washington
Vancouver Central Park Plan
Vancouver, Washington
1980

Merit Award
American Institute of
Architects, Arizona Society
(State Chapter)
Casas Adobes Post Office
Tucson, Arizona
1979

Honor Award
Department of Housing and
Urban Development
Freeway Park
Seattle, Washington
1979

**First Award, Community
Planning**
American Planning
Association, Washington
Chapter
Karluk Village Relocation Plan
Alaska
1979

Honorable Mention
American Planning
Association, Washington
Chapter
Tri-Cities Construction Impact
Study
Tri-Cities, Washington
1979

**Award of Merit, Community
Planning**
American Planning
Association, Washington
Chapter
Vancouver Central Park Plan
Vancouver, Washington
1979

Merit Award
American Institute of
Architects, Columbus Chapter
YMCA North Branch
Columbus, Ohio
1979

**American Institute of
Architects Honor Award**
Architects Society of Ohio
YMCA North Branch
Columbus, Ohio
1979

Honor Award
American Institute of
Architects, Anchorage Chapter
Cook Inlet Region, Inc.
Headquarters Office Building
Anchorage, Alaska
1978

First Award, Urban Design
American Planning
Association, Washington
Chapter
Interurban Corridor Study
Tukwila, Washington
1978

Merit Award
American Institute of
Architects, Arizona Society
(State Chapter)
Navajo County Governmental
Center
Holbrook, Navajo County,
Arizona
1978

Merit Award
American Planning
Association, Washington
Chapter
Quinault Valley Impact Study,
Washington
1978

Citation Award
American Institute of
Architects, Seattle Chapter
Salk Institute for Biological
Studies, Cancer Research
Animal Facility Addition
La Jolla, California
(in association with Deems/
Lewis & Partners, San Diego)
1978

**Special Commendation, Social
Planning**
American Institute of Planners,
Washington Chapter
Alaska Native Housing Study
1977

First Honor Award
American Institute of
Architects, Seattle Chapter
Children's Hospital and
Medical Center, Phase I
Addition
Seattle, Washington
1977

Landscape Award
Ohio Nurserymen's Association
Courthouse Square
Columbus, Ohio
1977

Special Award
American Institute of
Architects, Seattle Chapter
The Kingdome (King County
Stadium)
Seattle, Washington
1977

Honor Award
American Institute of
Architects, Seattle Chapter
Clarence D. Martin Stadium,
North Stands Replacement
Seating, Washington State
University
Pullman, Washington
1977

Honor Award
American Institute of
Architects, Seattle Chapter
Puget Sound Mutual Savings
Bank, West Seattle Branch
Seattle, Washington
1977

Merit Award
American Institute of
Architects, Tucson Chapter
University of Arizona Stadium
Addition
Tucson, Arizona (as
consultants to Finical &
Dombrowski, Tucson)
1977

Merit Award
American Institute of
Architects, Anchorage Chapter
Anchorage Air Mail Facility
Anchorage, Alaska
1976

City Beautiful Award
Columbus Convention and
Visitors Bureau
Courthouse Square
Columbus, Ohio
1976

Honor Award
American Institute of
Architects, Seattle Chapter
Reed, McClure, Moceri &
Thonn
1976

Merit Award
American Institute of
Architects, Columbus Chapter
Courthouse Square
Columbus, Ohio
1975

**Annual Environment Honor
Award, Preservation Category**
Environmental Monthly
magazine
Union Station Feasibility Study
Seattle, Washington
1975

National Design Award
General Services
Administration, Biennial
Design Awards Program
US Pavilion, Expo '74 General
Services Administration
Spokane, Washington
1975

**First Award for Vacation
Homes**
American Plywood Association
Admiralty Condominium, Pope
& Talbot
Port Ludlow, Washington
1974

Exhibition Award
American Institute of
Architects, Seattle Chapter
Bellevue Community College
Bellevue, Washington
1974

Honor Award
American Institute of
Architects, Seattle Chapter
The Financial Center, UNICO
Properties
Seattle, Washington
1974

Design Citation
Progressive Architecture
magazine
Sitka Indian Village
Redevelopment Plan
Sitka, Alaska
1974

Merit Award
American Institute of
Architects, Seattle Chapter
US Pavilion, Expo '74 General
Services Administration
Spokane, Washington
1974

Merit Award
American Institute of
Architects, Seattle Chapter
Bellevue Community College
Bellevue, Washington
1973

**Annual Environment Honor
Award, Land Use Category**
Environmental Monthly
magazine
Sitka Indian Village
Redevelopment Plan
Sitka, Alaska
1973

First Place Winner
Design Competition
Battelle Memorial Institute,
Academy for Contemporary
Problems
Columbus, Ohio
1971

Exhibition Award
American Institute of
Architects, Seattle Chapter
Business Space Design Offices
Seattle, Washington
1970

Merit Award
American Institute of
Architects, Seattle Chapter
College Club Office and Club
Building
Seattle, Washington
1970

First Place Winner
Design Competition
Honolulu Municipal Office
Building
Honolulu, Hawaii
1970

Honor Award
American Institute of
Architects, Seattle Chapter
Nordstrom Aurora Village
Seattle, Washington
1970

Honor Award
American Institute of
Architects, Seattle Chapter
1001 Fourth Avenue Plaza
Building
Seattle, Washington
1970

Excellence in System Design
US Department of Housing
and Urban Development
Seattle Comprehensive Transit
System Plan Concept
Seattle, Washington
1970

Honor Award
American Institute of
Architects, Northwest Region
Battelle Memorial Institute,
Seattle Research Center
Seattle, Washington
1969

**Citation, Home Design Awards
Program**
American Institute of
Architects/Sunset magazine
Gresham Residence
Tucson, Arizona
1969

**National Award for Superlative
Achievement in Interior Design**
Institutions magazine
Harbormaster Restaurant,
Pope & Talbot
Port Ludlow, Washington
1969

**Laboratory of the Year,
National Award**
Industrial Research and
Development magazine
Battelle Memorial Institute,
Northwest Research Center
Richland, Washington
1968

Design Citation
Progressive Architecture
magazine
Bellevue Community College
Bellevue, Washington
1968

Honor Award
American Institute of
Architects, Seattle Chapter
Cordiner Hall, Whitman
College
Walla Walla, Washington
1968

Design Citation
Progressive Architecture
magazine
Design Disciplines Building,
Washington State University
Pullman, Washington
1968

**Award for Progressive Airport
Beautification**
Federal Aviation
Administration
Guam Air Terminal
Island of Guam
1968

Merit Award
American Institute of
Architects, Seattle Chapter
Harbormaster Restaurant,
Pope & Talbot
Port Ludlow, Washington
1968

**Downtown Seattle "New Look"
Award**
Naramore Fountain
Seattle, Washington
1968

Merit Award
American Institute of
Architects, Seattle Chapter
Battelle Memorial Institute,
Seattle Research Center
Seattle, Washington
1967

**First Annual Highway Beauty
Award**
State Highway Department
Naramore Fountain
Seattle, Washington
1967

Art Achievement Award
Seattle Beautiful, Inc.
Naramore Fountain
Seattle, Washington
1967

Graphic Design Awards

Creativity 25
"King", Empty Space Theater
Poster; NBBJ Graphic Design
Self-Promotion
1995

**HOW's International Annual of
Design**
NBBJ Graphic Design Self-
Promotion; "Love and Anger",
Empty Space Theater Poster
1995

HOW Self Promotion
NBBJ Graphic Design Self-
Promotion; NBBJ Partners
Announcement
1995

Print's Regional Design Award
"Kin", Empty Space Theater
Poster
1995

**Type Directors Club,
"Typography 16"**
"Love and Anger", Empty
Space Theater Poster
1995

Aldus Magazine Design Contest
NBBJ After Hours Postcard
1994

Creativity 24
"Bumbershoot", "Someone
Who'll Watch Over Me", Empty
Space Theater Posters
1994

HOW Self Promotion
"Bumbershoot", Empty Space
Theater Poster; Oktoberfest
1993; Paramount Theater
Invitation and VIP Pass
1994

Print's Regional Design Award
"Mandragola Unchained",
Empty Space Theater Poster
1994

AIGA Magazine Design Contest
"Bumbershoot" Press Kit
1993

Aldus Magazine Design Contest
NBBJ Calendar 1993
1993

HOW Self Promotion
1991 San Francisco Open
House Invitation
1993

Aldus Magazine Design Contest
Sports Brochure, Retail/
Interiors Postcard Series,
Wedding Invitation
1992

Creativity 22
Theater Postcard Series,
Wedding Invitation
1992

Graphis Poster '91
"Etta Jenks", Empty Space
Theater Poster
1992

Seattle Design Association
NBBJ Christmas Party
Invitation, Marathon
Promotion Piece, Sports
Brochure, Wedding Invitation,
San Francisco Open House
1991 Invitation
1992

Aldus Magazine Design Contest
Empty Space Theater Poster
Series, Arizona Open House
Invitation, Christmas Party
Invitation
1991

Creativity 20
"Speed the Plow", Empty Space
Theater Poster
1991

Graphis Poster '91
"Etta Jenks", Empty Space
Theater Poster
Certificate of Merit, Collateral
Category
James River Corporation
Graphic Awards Competition
MacTac Label Awards
1990 San Francisco Open
House Invitation
1991

**Outstanding Invitations and
Announcements**
1990 Christmas Party Invitation
1991

**Society of Marketing
Professional Services**
Corporate Identity, 1990
Christmas Party Invitation
1991

Printing Industry of America
Officing in the Future; Retail
Concepts Brochure; "Speed the
Plow" poster
1990

Seattle Design Association
Tucson Open House; San
Francisco Open House; "Speed
the Plow" poster; "Etta Jenks"
poster; "Lost Formicans"
poster; Nine Proposal Covers
1990

Creativity '90
"Speed the Plow", Empty Space
Theater Poster
1990

Seattle Design Association
Tucson Open House; San
Francisco Open House; "Speed
the Plow" poster; "Etta Jenks"
poster; "Lost Formicans"
poster; Nine Proposal Covers
1989

Printing Industry of America
Retail Folder
1988

Design Award
Society of Marketing
Professional Services
1988

Seattle Design Association
Pasta & Co.
1987

Design Award
Society of Marketing
Professional Services
1986

Seattle Design Association
Culture and Perception Series
1985

Seattle Design Association
Culture and Perception Series
1983

Seattle Design Association
Culture and Perception Series
1981

Bibliography

Publications by NBBJ partners

William J. Bain, Jr., FAIA
"Rehabilitating A Building."
Property Newsline (Summer 1991).

"Discontinuities in Educational Facilities Design 1980." *College & University Business* (September 1990).

"The United States Pavilion."
Consulting Engineer (July 1974).

"Are Cities Doomed?" *Puget Sound Home Buyers Guide* (Fall 1968).

"Decision to Update" *Buildings* (June 1968).

Friedrich K.M. Böhm, FAIA
"Birth of a New Town." Co-author, *Ohio Cities and Villages* (1975).

"Revitalization of Downtown." Co-author, *Progress* magazine (1976).

"Revitalization of Downtown." Co-author, *Municipal Maryland* (1976).

James O. Jonassen, FAIA, MRAIC
"The Transition from 'Illness' to 'Wellness' Health Care." *Hospital Authority Newsletter* (June 1996).

"New Directions for Health Facilities: A Value-Driven View." *Journal of Healthcare Design* (August 1995).

"Design Strategies to Assist Healing." *Hospital Management International* (1995); *Asian Hospital* (March/April 1995).

"Health Care Architecture: Designs for the Future." Foreword to Lynn Nesmith's *Health Care Architecture*, Rockford Publishing, 1995.

"Healing By Design: Improving Health Care through Architecture." *Horizon Air* (January 1994).

"High Quality Health Focus Could Cure Ills of System." *Healthcare Strategic Management* (April 1991).

"The Future of Healthcare Architecture." *Healthcare Strategic Management* (July 1987).

"Hospital-Based Ambulatory Surgery: Two Case Studies." In Linda A. Burns' *Ambulatory Surgery: Developing and Managing Successful Programs*, 1984.

"The Current State of Surgical Suite Design in the US." *AIA Health Committee Newsletter* (September 1980).

"Life Cycle Cost: One Way to Help Get the Best Buy." *Hospital Forum* (July/August 1979).

"Life Cycle Cost: Using it in Practice." *AIA Journal* (March 1979).

"Adaptation of an Urban Site." *Journal of the American Hospital Association* (February 1974).

"Hospital Shared Facilities and the Area Industrial Zone." *Journal of the American Hospital Association* (January 1971).

John R. Pangrazio
"What Makes A Medical Office Building Competitive?" *Hospitals* (February 1982).

"Designing the Hospital-Based Medical Office Building." *Healthcare Financial Management* (November 1983).

Neil B. Anderson
"The Medical Office Building: A Strategic Key to the Future." *Trustee* magazine (February 1989).

Publications on NBBJ

1001 Fourth Avenue Plaza Building
Architectural Record (1970).

Applied Voice Technology
Interiors (February 1992).

Axelrod Condominium
Interiors (December 1993).

Bagley Wright Theater
Architectural Record (November 1984).
Architecture and Urbanism (May 1985).
L'Industria delle Construzioni (August 1985).
Vogue Decoration (June 1985).

Bannerworks
Architecture (August 1986).

Battelle Seattle Conference Center and Battelle Pacific Northwest Laboratory
L'Industria delle Construzioni (November 1984).

The Biomembrane Institute
Contract Design (September 1991).

Bogle & Gates
Lawyer/Manager (January 1990).

Brooks Brothers, Cleveland
Visual Merchandising + Store Design (May 1991).

Brooks Brothers, Tower City
Contract Design (July 1991).

Burger King Corp. Headquarters
Interiors (December 1994).

Cable Langenbach Henry Watkins & Kinerk
Interior Design (November 1988).
Washington Law (September/October 1990).

Canyon View Elementary School
Architecture (January 1991).

Carpenter Hall, WA State University
Building Operating Management (August 1993).
Building Renovation (July/August 1993).

Casper Events Center
Costruire (November 1984).

Central Ohio Technical College, Howard E. LeFevre Hall
World Architecture (no. 35, 1995).

Central Washington Hospital
Architecture (December 1992).
Chinese World Architecture (Summer 1995).
Nesmith, Eleanor Lynn. *Health Care Architecture Designs for the Future*, 1994.
World Architecture (no. 35, 1995).

Children's Hospital and Health Center, Patient Care Pavilion
Architecture (April 1993).
Architecture (July 1991).
Chicago Tribune (September 1993).
Chinese World Architecture (Summer 1995).
Designing for Child Health (Summer 1993).
Good Housekeeping (September 1993).
Healing Healthcare Network Newsletter (vol. 4, no. 2, 1993).
Health Care Strategic Management (May 1994).
Hospital Development (November 1993).
Institutional Architecture (1994).
Interiors & Sources (August 1993).
Interiors (December 1993).
Marberry, Sara. *Innovations in Healthcare Design*, 1995.
Modern Healthcare (November 1993).
Nesmith, Eleanor Lynn. *Health Care Architecture Designs for the Future*, 1994.
The New York Times (May 1993).
San Diego Magazine (February 1993).
The San Diego Union-Tribune (February 1993).
Tile Industry News (July/August 1993).
Tile World (September/October 1993).
World Architecture (no. 35, 1995).

Columbus State Community College, Harold M. Nestor Academic Center
World Architecture (no. 35, 1995).

CyberStation, Pier 39
Contract Design (July 1991).

Data I/O
Architectural Record (April 1984).

David Grant Medical Center, Travis Air Force Base
Institutional Architecture (1994).
James, Paul & Noakes, Tony. *Hospital Architecture*, 1994.
World Architecture (no. 35, 1995).

Davis Wright & Jones
Professional Office Design (January 1987).

DeMiguel Elementary School
Progressive Architecture (July 1991).

Eddie Bauer
Contract Design (July 1991).

Encore Entertainment
Visual Merchandising + Store Design (June 1992).

Ernst & Young (interiors)
Facilities Design & Management (October 1984).

Fluke Hall, University of Washington
Architecture (July 1991).
Seattle Daily Journal of Commerce (24 October 1990).
Seattle Daily Journal of Commerce (6 March 1991).
Seattle Post-Intelligencer (23 April 1990).
World Architecture (no. 35, 1995).

Four Seasons Olympic Hotel
Architectural Record (December 1982).
Designers West Magazine (December 1982).
Lodging Hospitality (January 1983).

Fuxing Mansion
Chinese World Architecture (Summer 1995).
World Architecture (no. 35, 1995).

Genesys Health Systems
Architecture (March 1993).
World Architecture (no. 35, 1995).

Graphics
Graphis Poster 91, The International Annual of Poster Art, 1991.
Outstanding Announcements, Invitations, and Greeting Cards, Art Direction Book Company, 1991.
Tucson Open House, NBBJ 1990 and 1991 Christmas Party Invitations, Spanish Serenade Invitation, 1991 United Way Fundraising Campaign. *Special Event Graphics,* 1992.

Great Northern Insured Annuity (Corporate Headquarters)
Interiors (January 1991).
Interiors (February 1990).
World Architecture (no. 35, 1995).

Gump's
Stores of the Year (1993).
Visual Merchandising + Store Design (June 1992).

Harrison Memorial Hospital
Interiors (February 1996).

Haworth Seattle Showroom
Interior Design (July 1986).

Heritage Building, NBBJ
Abitare (October 1984).
Architectural Record (May 1984).
Baumeister (October 1984).
Corporate Design (September 1984).
The Weekly, Seattle (February 1983).
World Architecture (no. 35, 1995).

Herman Miller Showroom
Interior Design (August 1996).

Herring/Newman
Contract Design (December 1993).
Northwest Design & Living (Summer 1993).
Seattle magazine (June 1994).

Hoedemaker Residence
Interiors (December 1994).

Honolulu Municipal Building
P/A Plans (March 1993).

Huang Pu District Central Hospital
Chinese World Architecture (Summer 1995).

Immunex Corporation
Designers West (February 1990).

Jay Jacobs
Visual Merchandising + Store Design (June 1992).

KeyArena
Architectural Record (February 1996).

Kimberly Woods
Modern Healthcare (October 1987).

King County Jail
Corrections Today (April 1985).
Progressive Architecture (March 1984).

The Kingdome
Abitare (October 1984).
L'Industria Delle Construzioni (1984).

Koo Foundation Cancer Center
World Architecture (no. 35, 1995).

Lamonts for Kids
Visual Merchandising + Store Design (June 1992).

Loma Linda University Children's Hospital
Building Design & Construction (March 1994).
Contract Design (June 1995).

Market Place Tower
Interiors (February 1992).
World Architecture (no. 35, 1995).

Menorah Campus
Progressive Architecture (May 1995).

Mercy Hospital Anderson [is this correct 'Mercy Hospital Anderson'?]
Sun Coast Architect/Builder (December 1994).

Merrill Place
Baumeister (October 1984).
Building Design and Construction (March 1985).

Miscellaneous
American Biotechnology Laboratory (July 1988).
Doors and Hardware (July 1988).
Health Care Strategic Management (July 1987).
Lab Animal (July 1988).

NBBJ
Building Design and Construction (September 1990).
Interiors (February 1992).
World Architecture (no. 35, 1995).

Nike, Inc. Office Interiors
Architecture (May 1991).
Interiors (June 1991).
Northwest Design & Living (Summer 1993).
Office Relocation (July 1994).

North Carolina Biotechnology Center
Architectural Record (May 1991).

North Carolina Indian Cultural Center, Visitors Center
Architecture (February 1991).

Northside Hospital Emergency Department Expansion and Renovation
World Architecture (June 1996).

Northwest Gallery of Fine Woodworking
Contract Design (July 1991).

Ocean Shipping Building
World Architecture (no. 35, 1995).

Old, Old Post Office
Professional Office Design (July/August 1987).

Palace Theater
Contract (August 1986).

Pasta & Co.
Abitare (1988).
Monitor (March 1988).
Restaurant and Hotel Design (October 1987).

Polo/Ralph Lauren
Visual Merchandising + Store Design (April 1994).

Pomona Valley Hospital and Medical Center, Women's Center
Architectural Culture (Korea, January 1996).
Architecture (March 1993).
Facilities Planning News (July 1992).
Nesmith, Eleanor Lynn. *Health Care Architecture Designs for the Future*, 1994.
World Architecture (no. 35, 1995).

Port Ludlow Resort—The Harbormaster Restaurant
Interiors (June 1969).

R.H. Johnson Memorial Stadium at Doubleday Field
Progressive Architecture (July 1995).

Rainbow Babies' and Children's Hospital, University Hospitals of Cleveland, Bed Tower Addition and Renovations
World Architecture (no. 35, 1995).

Resurrection Lutheran Church
World Architecture (no. 35, 1995)

Retail—Miscellaneous
Visual Merchandising + Store Design (May 1989).

Revco Drug Stores
Visual Merchandising + Store Design (June 1992).

Roswell Park Cancer Institute, Medical Research Complex
AIA Advanced Technologies Facilities Design Review (1996).

The Russell Building/Frank Russell Company
Interiors (February 1990).

Scottsdale Memorial Hospital North
Hospitals (October 1984).
James, Paul & Noakes, Tony. *Hospital Architecture*, 1994.
Progressive Architecture (March 1985).

Seafirst Gallery
Architecture (July 1994).
Progressive Architecture (April 1994).

Seattle-Tacoma International Airport, Concourse Improvements
Architectural Record (June 1993).
Building for Air Travel: Architecture and Design for Commercial Aviation (October 1996).
World Architecture (no. 35, 1995).

Simpson Investment Company
Interiors (February 1992).

Simpson Paper Company
Interior Design (May 1996).

Skagit County Jail
Northwest Architecture (November 1984).

Snyder Residence
Washington CEO (May 1992).

Squire Sanders & Dempsey Law Offices
Interior Design (November 1991).

St Andrew the Apostle Catholic Church
Interiors (February 1992).

St Francis Xavier Hospital
Health Facilities Management (October 1988).

Sun Mountain Lodge
Cross Country (October 1990).
Hospitality Design (November 1992).
Interiors (February 1992).
Interiors (January 1992).
Pacific Northwest (January 1990).
Seattle Post-Intelligencer (16 August 1990).
World Architecture (no. 35, 1995).

Swedish Medical Center, Southeast Wing Addition
Architecture (March 1993).
World Architecture (no. 35, 1995).

Three Nationwide Plaza
Modern Steel Construction (April 1989).

Tucson Arizona State Office Building
World Architecture (no. 35, 1995).

Two Union Square
Architectural Record (July 1990).
Architectural Record (May 1990).
Architecture (October 1990).
Architecture and Urbanism (February 1991).
Building Design and Construction (August 1990).
Building Design and Construction (January 1991).
Building Operating Management (August 1993).
Chinese World Architecture (Summer 1995).
Civil Engineering (October 1987).
Seattle Business (August 1989).
Seattle Daily Journal of Commerce (27 July 1988).
Seattle Times (16 July 1989).
Seattle Weekly (26 July 1989).
World Architecture (no. 35, 1995).

University of Arizona, College of Architecture
Interiors (February 1992).

University of California, Davis Medical Center, ICU Renovation
Northern California Medicine (1993).

University of California, Davis Medical Center, Medical Research Buildings I and II
Facilities Planning News (January 1993).
University Science Facilities (June 1993).
World Architecture (no. 35, 1995).

University of Washington, 4245 Roosevelt
Interior Design (March 1996).

University of Washington, Physics and Astronomy Building
Architecture (February 1995).
Columns: The University of Washington Alumni Magazine (September 1994).

US Pavilion, Expo '74
World Architecture (no. 35, 1995).

Walker Richer & Quinn, Incorporated
Interior Design (May 1996).

Weinberg/Menorah Campus
Progressive Architecture (May 1995).

Wexner Institute of Pediatric Research
Health Facilities Management (March 1989).

Williams-Sonoma, Westlake Center
Contract Design (July 1991).

Worthington Kilbourne High School
World Architecture (no. 35, 1995).

Wyatt Stapper Architects Firm Profile
Visual Merchandising + Store Design (April 1990).

Wyoming Women's Center
Architectural Record (April 1987).
Brick in Architecture (1984).
Corrections Today (April 1985).
Progressive Architecture (March 1984).

ZymoGenetics Corporate Headquarters
Architectural Record (February 1995).
Building Design & Construction (April 1995).
Building Design & Construction (December 1993).
Building Renovation (March 1995).
Facilities Planning News (September 1994).
World Architecture (no. 35, 1995).

List of Current Staff

James Adams
Gretchen Addi
John Adkins
Sean Airhart
Hassan Al-Zagha
Cam Allen
Ralph Allen
Mary Allen
Jonathan Allgaier
Daichi Amano
Mike Amaya
Leslie Ambrose
Mike Anderberg
Diane Anderson
Dorman Anderson
Eve Anderson
Neil Anderson
Sharon Anderson
Ed Andrews
Nancy Antonelli
Chris Appleford
Jarrod Arbini
Dohn Armon
William Auld
Jeffrey Bailey
Brodie Bain
William Bain, Jr.
Amy Baker
Daniel Ball
Michael Ball
Peter Bardwell
Michelle Basinger
Thomas Baty
Paul Becker
Derek Beecham
Philip Begley
Ralph Belton
Randy Benedict
Niranjan Benegal
Becky Benson
Brian Berg
Kimball Bergerud

Les Bergsman
Timothy Berical
Michele Bernardo
Patricia Beron
Brian Berson
Alfred Berthold
Bruce Best
Stephen Bettge
Wayne Biando
Steve Bobbitt
Friedrich Böhm
Mathew Bollen
Herbert Bondy
Bruce Bonine
Yuji Boraca
Brian Bowman
Patrik Bowman
Dennis Brandon
Barbara Breckenfeld
Jill Brengman
James Brennan
Richard Brennecke
Heather Briggeman
David Brindle
James Brinkley
Valerie Broadwin
Andy Bromberg
Judy Brooks
Shirlana Brooks
Shannon Brown
Barbara Brown
Kirstie Brown-Wirick
Timothy Brownlee
Robert Bruckner
Kimberly Brumfiel
Jeffrey Bryan
Steve Bryan
Jeff Bryan
Erica Buck
Richard Buckley
Ann Buratto
Kerry Burg

Dave Burger
Martha Burns
Laura Callahan
Dace Campbell
Kerrie Cardon
John Carr
Rosemary Carraher
Carlos Chang
Nick Charles
Stuart Charles
Elizabeth Cheatham
Jeffrey Chinberg
Michael Christoff
Steve Chung
Tarry Chung
Yi-Chang Chung
John Cleary
Ronald Clensy
Pam Coates
Stacy Cochran
Amy Cockburn
Daniel Cockrell
Donna Cofield
Josh Cohn
Kay Compton
Cathy Comstock
Elizabeth Conklin
Brian Connelly
Julie Cook
Richard Cook
Bernard Costantino
Foxie Cousins
Susana Covarrubias
Jeannine Crane
David Craven
Karen Cribbins-Kuklin
Marc Crichton
Anne Cunningham
Bradley Curtis
Mark Curtner
Katie Curva
Robert Czekner

Peter D'Amico
Bruce Dahlstrom
David Dahnke
Richard Dallam
Robin Dalton
Peter Damento
Tessie Dantes-Era
Marc Davidson
Donna Davis
Paul Davis
Ed Dean
Jeanette Dean
Joel Decker
Steven Defelippi
Steven DelFraino
Jennifer Demitruk
David Demus
Dan Dennison
Janene Desantis
Susan Dewey
Ronald Dickerson
Jeremy Diebert
Reidar Dittmann
Dana Dixon
Budy Djunaedi
Carla Doerr
Robert Dooley
Rebecca Dudley
David Duff
Pam Duren
Susan Durner
Mark Dye
James Dziatkowicz
Glenn Easley
Gary Edmonds
James Edson
Jessica Edwards
Eduardo Egea
Brian Eichenlaub
Thomas Eisele
Iman El-Bash
Quentin Elliott

Tori Engel
Sharon Englehart
Wade Entezar
Gabriel Esquivel
Shahram Etaat
Robert Faris
Cathe Farrington
Andrew FauntLeRoy
Sandy Felver
Angel Fernandez
Arnold Fernandez
Melanie Ferrini
Timothy Fishking
Sean Foley
Patrick Forgey
Dennis Forsyth
Thomas Fox
Linda Fuhr
Yumiko Fujimori
Mark Furgeson
Arthur Furukawa
E. Roko Gaal
Bruce Gallogly
Karl Gamertsfelder
Stephen Gawronski
Ellen Gehrlich
Nikolina Georgievska
John Geyer
Stephen Glen
Ruth Gless
Judith Glickman
Larry Goetz
Reuben Gonzalez
Kristi Gormley
Henry Goszytla
William Gragg
Lyn Grahn
Liz Granryd
Mark Grasmehr
Duncan Griffin
Thomas Grove
Grant Gustafson

Tanya Hagiwara
Denise Ha
Joy Hale
Bryan Hall
Cameron Hall
Douglas Hall
John Halleran
Michael Hallmark
Taylor Hamblett
Michael Hamilton
Ken Hamm
Knut Hansen
Craig Hardman
Jeffrey Harkey
Lisa Harrington
Gretchen Harriott
Cory Harris
Melissa Hartman
Beth Hartwick
Traci Hastings
Robert Hatfield
Cecile Haw
Kristin Hawk
Kerry Hegedus
Lawrence Helman
Nick Hendrickson
Jenny Hepperle
Joe Herrin
Kit Herrod
Karen Hillam
Dirk Hinnenkamp
Wayne Hiranaka
Allen Ho
Angeline Ho
James Hobbs
David Hoedemaker
Dana Hollingshead
Connie Holloway
Michael Hootman
Todd Hope
William Hopkins
Diane Horrell

Margaret Hoselton
Peter Houghton
Don Howe
David Huang
Lisa Hudson
Ryan Hullinger
Maureen Hylander
Jeanne Iannucci
Roxanne Ingoe
Jill Jago
Rhe Jain
Robert Jarc
Keith Jasinski
Pamela Jenkins
Joel John
Ann Johnson
Fritz Johnson
Scott Johnson
William Johnson
James Jonassen
Susan Jones
Marianne Jones
Ralph Jorgenson
Onah Jung
Richard Kanoski
Kimberly Karam
Tomomi Katagiri
Diane Kattine
Wayne Kaufman
Stephen Kaunelis
Brendan Kelly
Darren Kelly
Jeannette Kelly
Kathleen Kelly
Stephanie Kenney
Doug Keyes
David Kim
Fred Kimotsuki
Christopher King
James Kinney
Paula Kistler
Robert Klie

Rebecca Kleinbaum
Phil Klinkon
Chuck Kolb
Mary Koon
Steven Kopf
Elizabeth Kotzin
Jessica Kramer
Bryan Krannitz
Michael Kreis
Michael Kroll
Donald Kruckeberg
Christoph Kruger
Richard Kuhn
Dave Kutsunai
Arnulfo Lagasca
Sharon Lahr
Amy Lam
Robert Lane
Andris Lapins
Christopher Larson
Diane Lasko
Bradley Leathley
Tom Leddo
Dick Lee
Stephen Lee
Yunn-Tay Lee
Margaret Lehman
James Lehnert
William Lehtonen
John Lemr
Craig Leonard
David Leptich
Chris LeTourneau
Marta Leu
Jonathan Lewis
Jane Lieberth
Paula Lien
Bing Lin
Diane Lindberg-Nigh
Da-Wei Liou
Josh Litvack
Henry Liu

John Lodge
Greg Lombardi
Yuwei Ma
John MacAllister
Bruce Macon
Michelle Mahaney
David Mancino
Jennifer Mann
Lynne Manning
Franco Manno
Geoffrey Mansfield
Peter Marciano
Gregory Mare
Teresa Martin
Charles Martin
Mara Martinez
Christine Martini
Mike Matson
Ken Mattiuz
Patrick McAllister
Edward McCagg II
Sarah McCain
Kathryn McCollister
Steven McConnell
Jannine McDonald
Margaret McGrath
Mark McIntire
Sybil McKenna
Andy McPherson
Cathy McRoberts
Judy Medema
Daniel Meis
Edward Mendelson
Linda Menerey
Kirsten Mercer
Michelle Mercer
Robert Messmer
Brooke Michl-Smith
John Millard
Michael Miller
Brad Minogue
Richard Mitchell

Valerie Mitrione
Kierstin Moffat
Daniel Moon
David Moore
Michael Mora
Cynthia Moraza
Julia Morgan
Danis Morgan-
McDermott
Renee Morris
James Morrison
Richard Morse
Lisa Mullikin
Carl Muskat
Joey Myers
Tim Myhr
Sharon Nagel
Andras Nagy
Christopher Naughton
David Neiman
Dean Neuenswander
James Newby
William Nichols
Emily Noble
Carol Nordling
Lori Noto
Phillip Nussbaum
Steven O'Brien
Angela O'Brien-Ruff
Patrick O'Hare
Dennis O'Neill
Terrance O'Neil
Teri Oelrich
Ronald Olsen
Bahi Oreizy
Judi Orwig
Ann Osterfeld
George Ostrow
Bart Overly
Scott Overturf
Elias Pace
Stephen Paddock

Brenda Page	Stephen Rice	Sally Shiverdecker	David Swolgaard	Melinda Warren
John Pangrazio	Tina Riedell	Crystal Shook	Philip Szostak	Breton Washington
Ben Parco	Doug Rigg	Tina Simon	Jan Szupinski	Craig Watterson
Jin Ah Park	Chandra Risher	Vicki Simons	William Talbott	Jim Waymire
Mi Joong Park	Teresa Ritter	Jay Singh	Kyle Talbott	Francis Weaver
Charles Parks	Luis Rivera	Daniel Skaggs	Hideto Tanaka	Fred Weingand
Doug Parris	Cheryl Robinson	James Skog	Irene Tarczynski	Howard Weiss
Allen Patrick	Hayden Robinson	Raymond Skonce	Paula Tardiff	Kathleen Wenning
Robert Patricy	Bill Rodehaver	Ashley Slane	Jennifer Taylor	Jutta Westermann
D'Neka Patten	Brent Rogers	Jeffrey Slane	Bryan Tessner	Allen Whitaker
Joseph Pax	Michael Rogers	Scott Slotterback	Michael Thalbinh	Daniel White
Sara Pelone	Darryl Rogers	Catherine Smith	Gary Thatcher	Brent Whiting
Tien Peng	Joe Roseto	Christina Smith	Duncan Thieme	Rudy Widjaja
Lynn Perkins	Karl Rude	Daniel Smith	Barbara Thomas	Gregory Wieland
Mark Perry	Robert Rudeen	Keith Smith	Everett Thomas	Jonathan Wilch
Doren Peterson	Kevin Russell	Lori Smith	Gregory Thompson	Norma Williams
Josh Pettersen	Gary Rutledge	Peter Smith	Jeb Thornburg	Peter Williams
Jack Pettit	Derek Ryan	Jeffrey Snively	Gayle Thorne	Denise Wingo
Gordon Phillips	Peter Samarin	Rosemarie Snyder	Lisa Tilder	Karen Wiram
Pamela Phillips	Janet Samples	Janet Snyder-Beck	Hai Tran	Angela Wong
Shawn Pickerill	Matthew Sanders	Julie Somner	Bridget Treloar	Stephen Wood
Daniel Pickett	William Sanford	Phillip Soule	Peter Tsugawa	John Woods
Sherri Pickett	Michael Sankey	David Sova	Stephen Turk	Peter Wren
Patti Pierce	Leigh Sata	Amy Sparks	Ronald Turner	Nikki Wright
Pola Piper	Jane Saunders	Inger Staggs Yancey	Kent Usher	Scott Wyatt
Daniel Podoll	John Savo	Kevin Stevens	Andrew van Leeuwen	April Yang
Debbie Pomp	Karl Schantz	Carsten Stinn	John Truong	Brian Yansen
Anthony Poon	James Schirtzinger	Tim Stiles	Jeri Vaughn	Ching-Ya Yeh
Nicole Portieri	Melissa Schrock	Myron Stitt	Vince Vergel de Dios	Tom Yi
Vernon Pounds	Garreth Schuh	Lori Stoin	Karen Vickery	Jerry Yin
Peter Pran	William Schultz	Ed Storer	Gabrielle Vidal	Alan Young
Senath Rankin	Donald Schuman	James Strausbaugh	David Virtue	David Yuan
Tom Rasnack	Mary Ann Schwab	Scott Strome	Joseph Volpe	Mahnaz Zahiry
Wesley Ratliff	Marcel Schwarb	Dean Stump	William Wagner	Brian Zeallear
Leo Raymundo	Kathleen Scipione	Rysia Suchecka	Shannon Walcher	Stephen Zetts
Laurel Rech	Jerome Scott	James Suehiro	Lori Walker-O'Connor	Justin Zier
Charles Reed	Gregory Sekreta	Richard Summa	Thomas Walsh	Rick Zieve
Margaret Reed	Ronald Seman	Leigh Sutphin	Jonathan Walston	Mary Ziga
Martin Regge	Valishali Shah	Elizabeth Sutton	Yu Wang	David Zimmerman
Michael Rehder	Anne Shannon	David Swain	Weiguang Wang	Judith Zitsman
Joe Rettenmaier	Dixie Sheary	Rob Swartz	Jonathan Ward	Laura Zoerb
Jenney Rice	Bragdon Shields	Chris Swigert	John Ward	Brad Zylstra

Acknowledgments

The partners wish to acknowledge the confidence, support and inspiration of our many clients, some of whom have retained us for numerous projects since the inception of our practice.

We are deeply grateful to our staff of intelligent, energetic and determined professionals who share our aspiration for excellence and believe, with us, that it is possible to become the best design firm in the world.

Our best work is always accomplished in conjunction with the best consultants and the best contractors, and we gratefully acknowledge our debt to these vital members of the building team.

And finally, we are grateful to Erika Rosenfeld for so skillfully articulating NBBJ's design philosophy in her introduction to this book, "Designing Common Ground"; to David Duff for guiding the collection and preparation of work from our offices in Columbus, New York, and Raleigh; to Bobby Pressley for making many of the drawings and for helping to organize the process; to Gregory Baisden for his writing skills; to Sharon Nagel for finding and organizing most of the written material; to Melody Jacques for organizing the photography of all illustrated projects; and to David Swolgaard and his staff for their critical support.

We were pleased to be asked by Images Publishing to participate in this series and wish to express our appreciation to Paul Latham and Alessina Brooks for their courtesy, counsel, and support.

Associated Architects

Leo A. Daly
Seattle-Tacoma International Airport Concourse Improvements

APEC Consultants, Inc. and IPPR Design Institute
China Ocean Shipping Company Building (COSCO, Beijing)
EBH Bodi Tower

HeBei Provincial Architectural Design and Research Institute, Shanghai Branch
Fuxing Mansion

ECI/Hyer, Inc.
Alaska Native Medical Center

Payto Architects
Rainbow Babies' and Children's Hospital

Haigo Shen & Associates
Koo Foundation Cancer Center

Deems/Lewis & Partners
Salk Institute Cancer Research Center Addition

Daly & Associates
ZymoGenetics New Corporate Headquarters

The Gorder/South Group
University of Wyoming Environmental Simulation Facility and Wyoming Womens Center

Spencer & Spencer, Inc.
Harold M. Nestor Academic Center, Columbus State Community College

Burr Lawrence Rising + Bates Architects, P.S.
Shanghai American School

Streeter & Associates
New Pacific Northwest Baseball Park

HKS, Eppstein Uhen, Jenk Architecture, American Design, Inc., L.L. Kennedy
Miller Park

Maddox-NBD, Inc. Brubaker/Brandt
Charles J. Ping Student Recreation Center, Ohio University

Elkus/Manfredi
Pacific Place
Seattle, Washington
1997

Mitchell/Giurgola & Thorp Architects
In Joon Chung Architect
Suyoung Bay Conceptual Master Plan

Photography Credits

Peter Aaron/ESTO: 99 (3); 100 (5, 6); 101 (7); 103 (10)

Christopher Barone: 49 (3); 50 (5); 51 (6)

Battelle NW Photography Unite, Battelle Memorial Institute: 149 (3, 4)

Karl Bischoff: 23 (1, 3); 127 (2, 3)

Dick Busher: 25 (3–5); 27 (3); 28 (5, 6); 29 (7, 10); 192 (2); 193 (5)

David Curran: 32 (2)

Ted D'Arms: 193 (4)

Chris Eden/Eden Arts: 59 (3, 5); 60 (7)

Lumen/Steve Elbert: 170 (2); 171 (6, 7); 194 (1); 195 (5)

Brad Feinknopf: 205 (6)

John Griesen: 122 (2); 123 (3, 4)

Steve Hall/Hendric Blessing: 45 (5, 6); 46 (7); 47 (8); 157 (9)

David Hewitt/Anne Garrison: 110 (20; 111 (3, 4); 112 (6, 7); 114 (2); 115 (3); 116 (6); 117 (7, 8); 118 (9, 10); 119 (11); 120 (12); 121 (13); 153 (5); 182 (2); 183 (3); 184 (4, 5); 185 (6)

Fred Housel: 162 (1); 164 (5)

James F. Housel: 31 (5); 44 (2)

Art Hupy: 151 (3, 4)

Timothy Hursley: 33 (3); 34 (5); 35 (7); 36 (9); 37 (14); 38 (15, 16); 39 (17); 40 (18, 20); 41 (21); 42 (22, 23); 43 (25); 58 (2); 176 (2); 177 (3, 4); 178 (7); 179 (8)

Douglas Kahn: 172 (2); 173 (6); 174 (2); 175 (3, 4)

Steve Keating: 57 (8); 126 (7, 8); 136 (3); 137 (4, 6, 7); 197 (4); 216 (1, 2)

Jim Martin: 150 (2)

Russ Muir: 164 (6)

Chas R. Pearson: 21 (1, 2)

Robert Pisano: 89 (2, 3)

Chris Roberts: 61 (9)

Stephen Rosen: 60 (8); 163 (3, 4)

Randall Lee Sheieber: 188 (1, 3)

Gordon Shenck: 128 (2); 129 (5)

Chris A. Webber: 214 (2, 3); 215 (4, 5)

David Wakely: 161 (3)

Paul Warchol: 19 (1); 24 (2); 26 (2); 28 (4); 30 (1); 31 (4, 6); 45 (3); 52 (2, 5); 53 (6, 7); 54 (2); 55 (4); 56 (5–7); 90 (2); 91 (3); 92 (1–3); 93 (4); 94 (1); 95 (2–4); 104 (2); 105 (3, 5); 106 (6); 107 (7–9); 108 (10); 109 (11); 112 (5); 113 (8); 124 (2); 125 (5); 126 (6); 130 (2); 131 (3); 132 (7, 8); 133 (9); 134 (10–12); 135 13, 14); 145 (2, 3); 154 (2); 155 (3); 156 (7); 157 (8); 158 (11); 159 (15); 196 (3); 197 (6); 204 (3); 205 (4, 5); 210 (1, 2); 211 (1)

Robert Ward/Sandra Williams: 152 (2, 3)

Index

Bold page numbers refer to projects
included in Selected Works